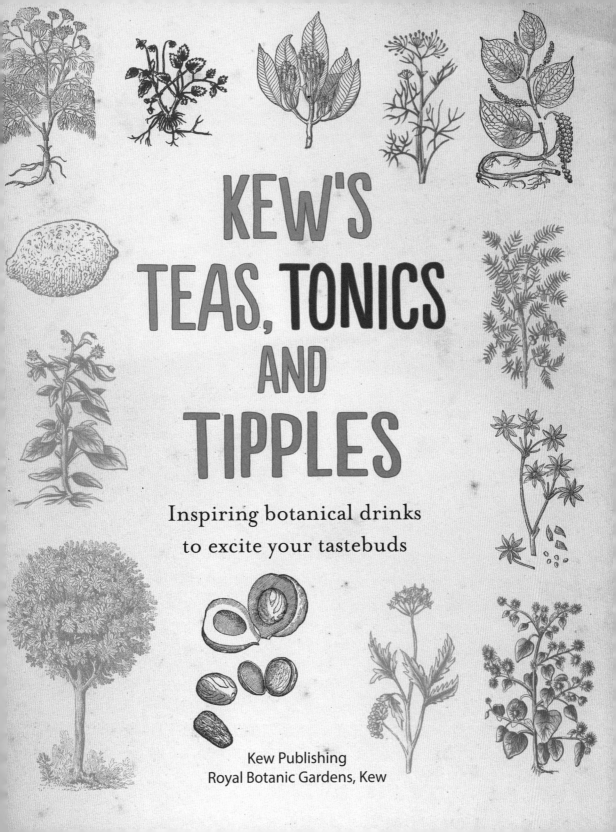

KEW'S
TEAS, TONICS
AND
TIPPLES

Inspiring botanical drinks
to excite your tastebuds

Kew Publishing
Royal Botanic Gardens, Kew

First published in 2015 by the Royal Botanic Gardens,
Kew, Richmond, Surrey, TW9 3AB, UK
www.kew.org
ISBN 978 1 84246 588 2

Distributed on behalf of the Royal Botanic Gardens, Kew
in North America by the University of Chicago Press,
1427 East 60th St, Chicago, IL 60637, USA.

British Library Cataloguing in Publication Data
A catalogue record for this book is available from the
British Library.

Project editors: Vanessa Daubney, Victoria Marshallsay
Photography: Paul Little, Thom Hudson
Copyediting and proofreading: Gina Fullerlove
Cover, text design and layout: Louise Millar
Production: Georgina Smith

Printed and bound by Printer Trento srl.
Holder of the following quality, printing and environmental certifications:
ISO 12647-2:2004
Fogra® PSO (Process Standard Offset)
CERTIprint®
ISO 14001:2004
FSC®(C015829)

For information or to purchase all Kew titles
please visit **shop.kew.org/kewbooksonline**
or email **publishing@kew.org**

Kew's mission is to inspire and deliver science-based plant conservation worldwide, enhancing the quality of life.

Kew receives about half of its running costs from Government through the Department for Environment, Food
and Rural Affairs (Defra). All other funding needed to support Kew's vital work comes from members, foundations,
donors and commercial activities, including book sales.

CONTENTS

Apple *(Malus)* from Duhamel du Monceau: *Traité des Arbres et Arbustes*, vol. 2, 1755.

INTRODUCTION

This book celebrates all kinds of drinks and the plants used to make them, along with their discovery, history and culture.

The liquids we drink not only sustain us, they are part of our culture. They refresh, invigorate and comfort us. Their consumption forms part of the daily habits and rituals that mark out our lives; we use them to celebrate, to remember and mourn.

Behind each drink there are stories of plants; their origin, histories of trading and cultivation. Many, like the grape vine, have been cultivated for longer than recorded history. Native to Caucasia, the vine is believed to have been grown by the Egyptians and Phoenicians 5,000 years ago. It was being grown in Greece by 2,000 BC, then in Italy and North Africa by about 1,000 BC. In the following 500 years it was cultivated in Spain, Portugal and the south of France, finally reaching northern Europe and Britain with the Romans.

Then there are the recipes themselves, passed down the generations. Some are ancient, many embrace specific traditions and cultures, even legends. In China 4,500 years ago, the Emperor Shennong was said to have been refreshed after drinking water boiled for him into which the leaves of tea (*Camellia sinensis*) had blown. In particular, sugar, herbs and spices emerged as key ingredients. In Europe, with its relatively poor native flora, the arrival of exotic fruits and spices must have been exciting. These reflect the history of exploration dating back to Columbus and the search for the 'spice islands'. The trading and caravan routes from east to west, known collectively as the Silk Road were important in bringing many edible plants to the west, including pistachio nuts and pears from West Asia, cucumber, apples, peaches and quinces from Central Asia, tea and rhubarb from China, and spices from India.

Star anise (*Illicium verum*) from Chaumeton: *Flore Médicale*, 1832.

Apple (*Malus*) from Redouté: *Choix des plus belles Fleurs et des Plus Beaux Fruits*, 1833.

Raspberry (*Rubus idaeus*) from
Redouté: *Choix des Plus Belles Fleurs
et des Plus Beaux Fruits*, 1833.

With this in mind we decided that we should create this book by asking colleagues and friends from the 'Kew community' to donate their favourite, original recipes. These have come from far and wide, such as ginger lemonade from a tropical botanical garden in Barbados visited by one Kew volunteer, to 'Norman Court Grog', passed from descendants of a ship's cook sailor to our senior conservator. We also have new drinks, for example, '20 Below', a homage to the juniper, seeds of which are stored at minus 20 degrees in Kew's Millennium Seed Bank (one of the most important global plant conservation projects ever undertaken). There are also recipes using green, herbal and fruit teas developed by a famous Yorkshire tea and coffee merchant, in partnership with Kew scientists.

To add perspective we have included eight short pieces by food and garden writers on a few of our most loved drinks and ingredients. Caroline Craig begins with beverages that mark our daily rituals; contributions from Hattie Ellis, Sarah Heaton, Bob Flowerdew and Sophie Missing cover three of Britain's favourites; teas, cider and gin, whilst Susanne Groom adds historic flavour with the drinking habits of the Georgian royals at Kew. Sheila Keating writes about chillies – a native of Mexico that now dominates cuisines worldwide. Finally, Jason Irving and Susanne Masters contribute pieces on bitters and on fennel – the 'spice of angels and seed of desolation'.

The Royal Botanic Gardens, Kew is home to the largest botanical collections in the world. Beautiful art, archival materials and artefacts from them have been used illustrate this book.

We hope you will enjoy reading and trying out many of the thirst-quenching recipes presented here. The key to success is to savour and use fresh ingredients, but also to be creative; don't be afraid to experiment and adapt the recipes to suit your taste.

GINA FULLERLOVE

The Moss Provence Rose by Ehret,
from Trew: *Hortus Nittidissimus*, 1750.

A HOT DRINK IN THE MORNING

by Caroline Craig

From the moment we wake to the final moments before sleep, our lives are bathed in ritual. Most of our actions subscribe to cultural norms, norms that are both a product of ever-fluid practices and our cultural histories. While we know that there are biological imperatives such as hunger and thirst that urge courses of action, the means, method and manner in which we act are informed by the culture in which we live.

Drinking practices are no different, and in western countries, though we might not think of them as rituals in the same vein as, say, the Japanese Tea Ceremony, they are rituals all the same, informed by our present culture, intrinsically created by years of human curiosity, design and exploitation around the globe: from the cup we drink from to the kettle we use to heat water in our indoor kitchens and the timing of the preparation.

There is perhaps nothing more universally appreciated than a hot drink. What varies across different cultures is the how, why, when and where they are taken. The curious anthropologist, tourist, or armchair traveller can derive much interest and even health benefits from observing, trying and adopting multifarious recipes and rituals from around the globe: a sweet chai in India to welcome visiting friends made with milk, black tea and blended spices, or in Provence, a luxurious café au lait, made with the dried, roasted cherries of *Coffea arabica* to stimulate the mind and body in the morning.

'Our cup is broken,' anthropologist Ruth Benedict reported Ramon, a so-called Digger Indian, as uttering at the turn of the 20th century in North America. A metaphor Benedict took to signify that the interruption and abrupt impact of the European presence had in a sense shattered his own, indigenous culture. Ramon's sadness is heart wrenching, and while we have lost much of the secrets and knowledge of his

A mate cup with drinking tube from the Kew's Economic Botany Collection.

Vanilla (*Vanilla planifolia*) from Régnault: *La Botanique Mise à la Portée de Tout le Monde*, 1774.

Compressed flowers from the tea plant (*Camellia sinensis*).

Lemon
Citrus x limon

A tea brick brought back by Joseph Hooker from India and now in Kew's Economic Botany Collection.

people, some wisdom has survived, such as the gathering and preparation of greenthread or Hopi tea. Made from the dried leaves of *Thelesperma megapotamicum* or *Thelesperma filifolium*, it is taken for its purported medicinal as well as soothing properties.

In these few words, I look at some of the imbibing rituals and pauses that punctuate my mornings, and metaphorically at least, read the tea leaves and look for some meaning and cultural context beyond their immediate thirst-quenching properties.

My days begin with a warm water and lemon at my kitchen table. The lemons we purchase from our greengrocers today are the fruits of commercially-grown, *Citrus* x *limon* hybrid trees. The parent species is thought to have originated from India, which could explain their prominence in Ayurvedic medicine. According to this ancient practice, a hot water and lemon is said to purify and cleanse the digestive system. The beautiful fruit's high vitamin C content also made it an effective treatment for sailors suffering from scurvy, though its use for this purpose was not widespread. The history of the spread of citrus fruit, and particularly lemons, throughout the world makes for romantic reading, and now we closely associate them with Italy where it is thought that varieties have been cultivated for more than 2,000 years.

The lack of caffeine in this virtuous start to my day means that by the time I arrive at work I make a beeline for the office kitchen and prepare a cup of tea, most often a Lapsang Souchong (made from the leaves of *Camellia sinensis* smoked over pinewood fires). Tea is so loved and much has been written on the subject: from its botanical and sociological origins as a luxury product from China to our adoption of that practical American invention, the tea bag, and endless debates on how to prepare the perfect brew. On the latter subject, George Orwell offered some sound advice in his 1946 essay 'A Nice Cup of Tea'. He exclaimed that tea should always be made in a teapot (warmed, naturally). And, in a bold statement that I thoroughly support, he maintained that 'a strong cup of tea is better than twenty weak ones'. While I am unlikely to bother with a teapot ahead of a Tuesday morning team meeting during the 9.00 am

office-kitchen rush hour, I will always endeavour to brew my tea to the requisite strength. I empty the kettle of any dregs, then fill it with fresh water from the tap. Once boiling, I pour the water over the Lapsang teabag, in my preferred vessel — a green, wide-brimmed French coffee bowl. The distinctive smoky smell floats from the cup and fills the room. It is not to everyone's taste, and I have often heard Lapsang referred to 'bacon' or 'sausage' tea. But I do love it, and so, apparently, did Winston Churchill.

For many, the later, mid-morning chime of 11.00 am signifies a coffee break, and 'it being an acknowledged fact that French coffee is decidedly superior to that made in England' (according to Mrs Beeton at least), the French cafétière is my method of choice for brewing *Coffea arabica* beans. It is a stimulating drink that keeps my office and, indeed, the world running both in the economic and physiological sense: From its botanical origins in Ethiopia and traces of cultural uses in ancient Yemen, today coffee is the most traded commodity after crude oil and its industry is estimated to employ 26 million people in 52 countries. Scientists at the Royal Botanic Gardens, Kew have highlighted the plant's sensitivity to climate change and the need to look to its wild relatives for genetic traits to improve species resilience to stress. The UK has seen more and more public houses closing in recent years, and coffee drinking outlets appear to be growing. However, there is something immensely pleasing about preparing one's own coffee; grinding the beans, heating some milk to enjoy it with, choosing a cup, the warm aroma rising... As the centuries roll by, pausing for a hot drink in its many forms will surely continue and there is something immensely comforting about that.

Coffee (*Coffea arabica*) from Plenck: *Icones Plantarum Medicinalium*, 1788–1812.

TEAS AND TISANES

Women Gardeners drinking tea at Royal Botanic Gardens, Kew, 1939. A tea break was only instigated at Kew after Minnie Hill made a personal appeal to the director, Sir Arthur Hill, and just ten minutes each afternoon was allowed.

Women gardeners were employed at Kew during World War II. Fourteen were enrolled onto the staff in 1940, joined by a further thirteen in 1941. The women referred to their uniform of apron and clogs as 'battledress'. The clogs were wooden soled shoes with leather uppers. One of the women, Jean Thompson told colleague Betty Cooper: 'My most vivid impression was the difficulty I had balancing on the rocks in my clogs.'

Camellia sinensis by unknown artist from the Company School, dating from late 18th century.

VANILLA CHAI

Chai is a creamy, sweet, spiced tea drink from India. Used in Ayurvedic medicine, many chai spice ingredients are included for their purported medicinal as well as aromatic properties. From ubiquitous chai street sellers to family homes in India, recipes vary and are often closely guarded family secrets, passed down through the generations. So do experiment with the spice mix below to create your own signature tea.

1. Remove the cardamom seeds from the pods and crush them along with the cloves using a pestle and mortar or the end of a rolling pin and a small bowl. Slice open the vanilla pod and scrape out the seeds using a sharp knife.

2. Place the cardamom and clove mixture, as well as the vanilla pod seeds and the remaining ingredients in a spouted saucepan over a low heat. Stir the mixture occasionally and bring it slowly to the boil.

3. Strain the tea, and serve immediately with sugar cubes.

Serves 6–8

3 **cardamom pods**

3 **cloves**

1 **vanilla pod**

1 tsp freshly ground **black pepper**

1 tsp ground **ginger**

¼ tsp **cinnamon**

1 **star anise**

4 **black teabags**, or 4 tsp of **black tea leaves**

600ml (1pt) whole **milk**

150ml (5fl oz) **water**

sugar cubes, to serve

Vanilla (*Vanilla planifolia*) from Köhler: *Medizinal Pflanzen*, 1883-1914.

Star anise
Illicium verum

MASALA CHAI

Bay (*Laurus nobilis*) imparts a wonderful fragrance to this delicious, gently spiced beverage. Bay plants are relatively easy to grow and a small, potted plant will be quite happy on a sunny windowsill, ready for you to pluck a leaf or two as required. Dried bay leaves hold their flavour very well and can be rather potent, so use just half a dried leaf in this recipe if fresh leaves are unavailable.

1. Pour the water into a large saucepan and set over a medium heat. Add the spices, bay leaf and grated ginger and bring to the boil. Turn off the heat and allow the mixture to infuse for 4–5 minutes.

2. Bring the water back to the boil and add the tea and sugar. Reduce the heat and simmer very gently for 2–3 minutes. Add the milk to the saucepan (the tea should be a light caramel colour, so add a little more tea if a stronger brew is required) and bring to the boil again.

3. Simmer gently for a further 5 minutes. Then take the saucepan off the heat and strain the tea into small tea glasses.

Serves 4

500ml (17fl oz) **water**

1 **cinnamon stick**, broken in half

6 green **cardamom pods**, cracked

4 **cloves**

8 **black peppercorns**, roughly crushed

1 fresh **bay leaf**

3cm (1¼in) piece **root ginger**, peeled and grated

300ml (½pt) whole **milk**

2 tbsp **black tea** leaves, or to taste

3 tsp **sugar**, or to taste

Bay (*Laurus nobilis*) from Sibthrop and Smith: *Flora Graeca*, vol. 4, 1823.

Clove
Syzygium aromaticum

ORANGE OR LEMON & MINT TEA

For a refreshing alternative to conventional tea, why not try this simple combination of refreshing mint and oranges or lemons.

Serves 2

a slice of **orange** or **lemon**

1 **cinnamon stick**

a small handful of fresh
    mint leaves

1 tsp of **honey**

1. Put the orange or lemon slice in a small teapot, and add the cinnamon stick and fresh mint.

2. Pour in boiling water and allow the mint, fruit and cinnamon to infuse. Then pour into a cup and sweeten with the honey.

Cinnamon (*Cinnamomum verum*) from the Roxburgh Collection.

Orange
Citrus x aurantium

MINT TEA

Jon Drori is a Trustee of the Royal Botanic Gardens, Kew and has been visiting the Gardens since he was a child. This is his family's favourite recipe for mint tea.

Serves 4

1 teabag or heaped tsp
    black tea

a generous handful of
    fresh mint leaves

boiling water

4 tsp **sugar**, or to taste

rose water, a drop (optional)

1. Place the tea or teabag in a teapot together with the mint and sugar. If making for the first time, you can omit the sugar and add it once the tea has been poured, according to your taste, or use a little sugar at this stage and then add more later, as desired.

2. Pour in the boiling water, stir and leave to infuse for three minutes. Strain the tea into four cups and serve, adding extra sugar if required.

LEMON BALM & MINT TISANE

This lovely tisane is very calming according to Jon Drori, so perfect after a frazzled day at the office. The ratio of lemon balm (*Melissa officinalis*) to mint leaves should be about 2:1.

1. Place the lemon balm and mint sprigs in a large mug.
2. Then pour in the boiling water, so that the leaves are covered.
3. Stir and leave for a couple of minutes to infuse. Then serve.

Serves 1
2 sprigs of **lemon balm**
1 sprig of **mint**
boiling **water**

Lemon balm (*Melissa officinalis*) from Hayne: *Getreue Darstellung und Beschreibung der in der Arzneykunde Gebräuchlichen Gewächse*, 1809.

MINT & FENNEL TISANE

Another favourite the Drori household, recommended for its restorative effects, to help settle a stomach ache. All the ingredients are known for their carminative effects and just watching it being prepared brings some comfort. Children particularly like it, but may prefer a little sugar to sweeten it.

1. Place the fennel seeds, cumin seeds and caraway seeds in a pestle and mortar and bruise them to help release their flavour. Alternatively, use the end of a rolling pin and a small bowl.
2. Place the seed mixture and mint leaves in a pot with a little sugar, as desired. Pour in about two mugfuls of boiling water. Stir the mixture and allow it to infuse for 3 minutes.
3. Using a tea-strainer, pour the tea into two mugs and add sugar as required to sweeten, and serve. Sip gently, but don't drink it if the tea is scalding hot – allow it to cool a little.

Serves 2
2 tsp **fennel seeds**
1 tsp **cumin seeds**
1 tsp **caraway seeds**
12 **mint leaves**
boiling **water**
sugar, to taste

Fennel
Foeniculum vulgare

BEE BALM BREW

Bee balm (*Monarda fistulosa, M. didyma*) became a popular staple with European settlers in America following the Boston Tea Party, when access to English tea was lost. A member of the mint family, it is a medicinal plant, thought to be useful in the relief of inflammatory conditions, such as colds and sore throats, but it also makes a useful after-dinner digestive. Stevia is a natural fruit sugar that is extracted from the stevia plant, and you only need a very small amount to achieve a good balance of flavour.

Makes 1 large mug

1 tbsp **bee balm** flower
   petals, freshly picked

150ml (5fl oz) boiling **water**

stevia, to taste

1. Put the bee balm flower petals in a small, warmed teapot, pour over the boiling water and leave to steep or infuse for a couple of minutes.

2. Strain the tea into a large mug. Sweeten it with a drop or two of stevia, and savour.

LEFT: Stevia (*Stevia rebaudiana*) from W. J. and J. D. Hooker: *Icones Plantarum*, 1906. RIGHT: Bee balm (*Monarda didyma*) from the Kew Collection.

MIDSUMMER'S NIGHT TISANE

The evocative aroma of roses conjures diverse images, from sultry Arabian nights to demure English-garden afternoon teas. Whether used in intensely flavoured sticky confections, such as Turkish delight, or a simple, delicate tisane, such as the one below, make the most of this summer beauty and include it in your culinary repertoire from June to September.

1. Rinse the rosebuds under cold, running water. Then place them in a warmed teapot.
2. Fill the pot with freshly boiled water and allow the rose tea to infuse for 5 minutes. Using a strainer, pour the tea into small, china teacups.
3. Serve with a dash of orange blossom honey to sweeten.

Serves 4
a handful of **Damask rose***
   buds, freshly picked
boiling **water**
orange blossom honey,
   to taste
*Rosa x *damascena*

LEFT: Damask rose (*Rosa* x *damascena*) from Lawrance: *A Collection of Roses from Nature*, 1799.
RIGHT: Orange blossom (*Citrus sinensis*) from Redouté: *Choix des Plus Belles Fleurs et des Plus Beaux Fruits*, 1833.

La Pensée.

Viola tricolor

P. J. Redouté

Langlois.

ZESTY PINK GRAPEFRUIT AND PANSY TEA

This tea can be sweetened, if desired, but the fresh, citrus qualities of pink grapefruit make it an ideal breakfast drink just as it is. Pansies or tiny violas (*Viola* spp.), particularly in shades of pink or purple, look lovely and add a very delicate flavour to the tea.

1. Put the pared grapefruit zest and juice into a warmed teapot. Add the boiling water.
2. Place a few pansy petals in each of four warmed teacups. Pour over the grapefruit tea and serve.

Serves 4

pared zest and juice of 2 large
pink grapefruits
500ml (18fl oz) boiling **water**
petals from 6–8 **pansy** heads

Grapefruit (*Citrus* x *aurantium*) from Risso and Poiteau: *Histoire et Culture des Orangers*, 1782.

HOW THE BRITISH FELL IN LOVE WITH TEA by Hattie Ellis

Tea isn't just a drink to the British; it's part of our national character. After the outbreak of war in 1939, the government moved tea stocks to warehouses outside London because a bombed brew would have inflicted such a devastating blow to our morale. Mealtimes, food and etiquette have all evolved around tannic tea. But how did a drink originating in China, made from the leaves of the exotic plant *Camellia sinensis* develop such a grip on the country's psyche? Other countries ultimately preferred coffee, but the British chose cups of black tea served with milk and often sugar. Why?

Growing tea, 1887.

When it first arrived in Britain in the mid 17th century, tea was an exotic import, seen as medicinal as much as a beverage, and was sold by apothecaries as well as the new coffee shops. It was Catherine of Braganza who made tea fashionable when she married King Charles II in 1662. A chest of China tea was part of her dowry, and her daily drink became integral to the elegance of court life. Tea was drunk from fine china, and soon acquired an entourage of etiquette and furniture such as tea tables. The lady of the house brewed and served the tea herself, and the precious leaves were kept in finely crafted caddies, some with a lock.

Packing tea in India.

The relationship of the British with tea is entwined with international trade and empire. In 1600, Queen Elizabeth I granted a charter to the British East India Company to trade with India and the Far East. Cargoes of the East India tradesmen contained tea along with spices, silks and porcelain, and the Company issued propaganda on behalf of the drink, partly to overcome the initial suspicions that this foreign import would supplant good honest British beer. At the end of the 17th century and the start of the 18th, England and Holland were at war with France and then also with

Visitors to Kew take tea at
the Refreshment Pavilion,
opened in 1920.

Harvesting tea leaves, India.

Men laden with 'Brick tea' for Tibet. Photograph taken by the plant-hunter Ernest Wilson, July 30, 1908.

Spain in the War of the Spanish Succession. In *A Social History of Tea*, Jane Pettigrew says that supply routes of coffee from the Levant were less certain than the tea from the East India Company.

Initially, the British drank more green tea than black. The latter was then called 'Bohea' tea, named after the mountains in China where it is still produced. But during the 18th century, black teas took over. Roasted black teas would certainly have survived the long journey from China better than the fresh green ones. Adding milk also became more commonplace, partly because it was seen as a fortifying, healthy substance, further boosting the health-giving aspect of tea, but also because it softened black teas, working less well with green ones. In the 18th century, sugar imports also soared. Some think the British thirst for tea went hand in hand with a near addiction to sweetness. It's even been suggested that we drank more black tea in order to consume more sugar, because sugar, as well as milk, softened the more tannic nature of black tea.

To begin with, tea was highly taxed and an expensive luxury restricted to the wealthy. But smuggling became endemic, and the drink spread through society in the 18th century. Unfortunately, adulteration was also common in this illegal trade. Other leaves, such as hawthorn, ash, elder and sloe, were passed off as 'tea' and fake green teas were coloured with copper compounds, making them harmful as well as counterfeit, another possible reason why we became firmly a nation of black tea drinkers.

Eventually, the government saw that it could not fight a national passion. In 1784, the Commutation Act cut tax from 119 per cent to 12 per cent. By this time, tea drinking had moved from being an afternoon or evening event to become part of breakfast, too, instead of alcohol. Samuel Johnson, in a famous defence of tea drinking, said he was one 'who with tea amuses the evening, with tea solaces the midnight, and with tea welcomes the morning'.

As people started eating dinner at a later hour, a hungry gap opened up in the afternoon. Afternoon tea, with its own dainty foods, became a drawing-room social occasion that was an established part of Victorian society. The trends of the teacup continued to be bound up with trade and Empire. In 1834, the East India Company lost its monopoly on trade with China and plantations were established in India and elsewhere to meet national demand. Tea supplies became more widespread and cheaper, and by the 1920s, around 60 per cent of world tea exports ended up in Britain.

By then, everyone drank tea. Some historians argue that the Industrial Revolution was partly fuelled by tea rather than beer, which was safe from the risk of disease but alcoholic, because the working man drank tea that was made safely with boiled water and gave the workforce energy as well as health. Household servants often had a tea allowance as part of their wages, and tea could be included as part of the 'downstairs' day, the early origins of the tea break.

At every step, tea infused culture and fashions. Teashops became part of national life after the first one was opened by the Aerated Bread Company (ABC) chain of bakery shops in 1864, starting an institution that thrives today. Tea dances came into vogue in the early 20th century, as did tea gowns for informal entertaining.

Just as the spices brought to Britain by the East India Company are still in the kitchen, tea is part of life. When Catherine of Braganza first set foot on British soil in Portsmouth, it is said that she asked for a cup of tea. Truth or myth, this strikes a deep chord. Coming back from work, a slog through the shops, a long walk, a beach swim or a hard afternoon's gardening, we reach for 'the cups that cheer but not inebriate'. The refreshing and restoring thought of a cuppa is decidedly part of Britain's 'national DNA'.

ABOVE: Tibetan teapot collected by Joseph Hooker on his Himalayan expedition 1847-49.

BELOW: Tea and coffee by J.J. Grandville from *Les Fleurs Animees*, Paris, 1847.

THÉ ET CAFÉ

Coffee (*Coffea arabica*) by Manu Lal,
Company School Drawing, 19th century:

Coffea Arabica

HOT WINTER WARMERS

WARM MOCHA PUNCH

Coffee can be far more than cappuccino or espresso. Its flavour, smooth and slightly bitter, has a great affinity with chocolate and has become popular across the world. Here Jeremy Cherfas combines chocolate, black coffee and coffee liqueur with cinnamon for a wonderfully spicy drink.

Serves 1–2

150ml (1/4pt) full fat **milk**

1 tbsp **drinking chocolate**

150ml (1/4pt) freshly brewed
   coffee

2 tbsp **coffee liqueur**

1 tbsp **sugar**

To serve:

a little **whipping cream**

a little grated **chocolate**

1 or 2 long **cinnamon sticks**

1. Warm the milk and whisk in the drinking chocolate, then combine with the coffee, liqueur and sugar to taste.

2. Whisk until frothy, then pour into glasses. Top each glass with a small dollop of lightly whipped cream, sprinkle with chocolate and serve with a cinnamon stick in each as a stirrer.

Cinnamon
Cinnamomum verum

Coffea (*Coffea arabica*) by Régnault: *La Botanique Mise à la Portée de Tout le Monde.* 1774.

TRIPLE C

Green cardamom is an intensely aromatic and resinous spice from the ginger family Zingiberaceae. Its strong, distinctive taste is widely known as a great complement to coffee. Jeremy Cherfas's recipe blends both pod and bean with cognac for a powerful and stimulating beverage.

1. Warm all the ingredients gently in a small saucepan for about 5 mins to allow the flavours to infuse. Serve. Vodka and grappa also work well in this coffee.

Serves 1

150ml (¼pt) freshly brewed **black coffee**

1–2 tsp **sugar** or more, to taste

2 **green cardamom pods**, bruised

1 tbsp **cognac** or more, to taste

Green cardamom (*Elettaria cardamomum*) from Köhler: *Medizinal Pflanzen*, 1883–1914.

MRS BEETON'S COCOA

This recipe from one of the doyennes of domestic cookery is more about technique than ingredients. It is very adaptable to personal taste and makes a good basis for variations that use additional tots of brandy or whisky, or different types of chocolate.

Serves 1

2 tsp **cocoa** or 1 tsp **cocoa essence** (per cup)*

300ml (10fl oz) **milk** or **water** (or a combination of both)

1. Put the cocoa in the cup. Pour over 4 tsp of the milk or water, and stir to make a paste.
2. Pour the remaining milk and/or water into a small saucepan, and heat until boiling. Then add the boiling milk and/or water to the chocolate paste. Stir for 1–2 minutes.

*Rock cocoa (10g/½oz) can be used in the same manner.

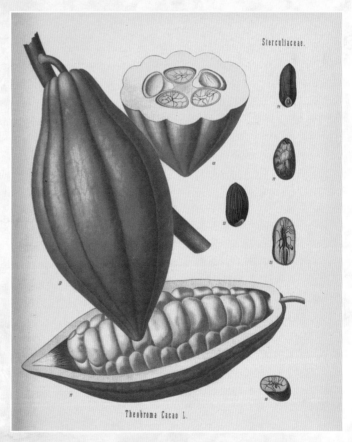

Cacao (*Theobroma cacao*) from Köhler: *Medizinal Pflanzen*, 1883–1914.

CHILLI HOT CHOCOLATE

The ancient Mayan and Aztec people revered both chocolate and chilli, so the ultimate experience was to bring both together in a heady, spicy drink. When Europeans started adapting these drinks to their taste during the Chocolate House craze in the 17th century, they would add other spices. So if you like, you can replace the chilli with a cinnamon stick and a vanilla pod while heating the cacao and water, then remove them before whisking.

1. Put all the ingredients in a saucepan. Bring to the boil, stirring frequently. Then lower the heat to a gentle simmer for around 3 minutes, or until the mixture thickens and becomes glossy.

2. With a hand whisk or, ideally, a stick blender, whisk the mixture well to create a light foam. Either drink the chocolate while hot, or if you want to serve your chocolate Aztec-style, leave it to cool to room temperature.

Serves 6

100g (3½oz) 100% **cacao**, roughly chopped

1 tsp **chilli powder,** to taste

¾ tsp **achiote powder** (optional)

2 tbsp raw **cane sugar**

450ml (¾pt) **water**

'CHOCOLATE in its purest form contains the so-called 'bliss molecule', sending messages to make you feel happy, so combining cacao and chilli gives you the ultimate, dynamic pick-you-up drink,' says chocolate afficionado Willie Harcourt-Cooze, who produces his 100 per cent Willie's Cacao cylinders slowly in small batches, using specially chosen beans and antique machinery at his Devon chocolate factory. 'For the hot chocolate, I use quite a mild chilli powder which helps to open up the flavours of the cacao, but you can experiment with hotter ones to suit your mood.' While some spicy chocolate recipes involve milk, Willie advocates the authentic drink made with water, and the simple combination of chocolate, chilli and achiote, as it is known in Mexico, or 'annatto' in the Caribbean. This is the spice made from the seeds of the tropical *Bixa orellana* shrub that the Aztecs are believed to have used to add a rich, red colour to their chocolate drinks. Annatto is the natural colouring also used by makers of traditional golden coloured cheeses, such as Double Gloucester and Red Leicester.

QUEEN CAROLINE, the wife of George II, enjoyed nothing better for breakfast than a cup of hot chocolate with a bowl of strawberries. When at her summer home at Richmond Lodge, she often took her breakfast in the company of her favourite lady in waiting, Lady Sundon, walking to her house in Kew along the riverside terrace. The Queen's cup of chocolate would be served to her from a silver pot, fitted with a moulinette or whisk, which could be twizzled to froth the liquid. Sometimes, spices such as cinnamon or vanilla were added to mask the inherently bitter taste of the chocolate. In Queen Caroline's kitchen, the cook had to start from a cocoa pod, but we can begin by merely snapping off a square of fine chocolate.

CAUDLE was traditionally drunk from two-handled cups. Josiah Wedgwood presented Queen Charlotte with a caudle and breakfast set on the birth of the future George IV in 1762, significantly boosting sales of his cream ware, which he shrewdly re-branded as 'Queen's ware'. There are numerous recipes for caudle, some adding small amounts of oatmeal, with mace, nutmeg and saffron or raisins and orange flower water as flavourings. The recipe for caudle on p33 is from *The Compleat Housewife or Accomplish'd Gentlewoman's Companion* (1753).

EIGHTEENTH-CENTURY-STYLE CHOCOLATE

Chocolate was certainly to the taste of royalty from the late 17th century, when William III employed his own chocolatier, Mr Nice, to make his favourite drink. Queen Anne acquired a liking for it, too, and after her reign, the Hanoverians continued to indulge in chocolate.

1. Put the chocolate and port, wine or sherry in a medium-sized saucepan and heat slowly, adding the sugar, to taste.
2. Whisk in a very small quantity of flour. Do not allow the mixture to boil.
3. Add the vanilla or cinnamon as desired. Continue whisking until the chocolate is frothy, and serve hot.

Serves 2

25–50g (1–2oz) **dark chocolate**, broken into pieces

½ bottle of **port, sherry** or **wine**

2–3 tbsp **caster sugar**

a pinch of fine **sauce flour**

1–2 drops of **vanilla essence** or ½ tsp **ground cinnamon** (optional)

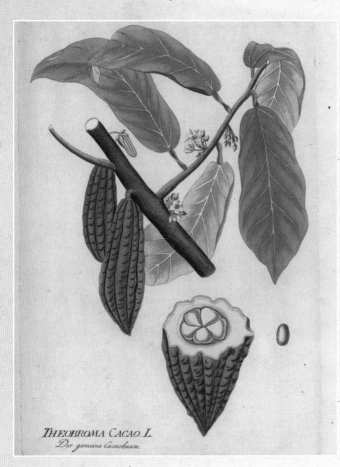

THEOBROMA CACAO. L.
Der gemeine Cacaobaum.

ABOVE: Cacao seeds from the Kew's Economic Botany Collection.

LEFT: Cacao (*Theobroma cacao*) from Plenck: *Icones Plantarum Medicinalium*, 1788–1812.

ELDER ROB

Kew botanist Lee Davies got this recipe from a friend years ago when he was visiting her and had come down with a cold. It is packed with vitamin C and is nice and syrupy so very soothing for sore throats and is generally very tasty.

Makes approximately 450ml (16 fl oz)

500g (1lb) **elderberries**
450g (15oz) **caster sugar**
300ml (½pt) **dark rum**

1. Put the elderberries in a saucepan with just enough water to cover them, simmer for half an hour or so, and mash them up a bit.

2. Strain the liquid into another saucepan and add 450g (15oz) of sugar for every 500ml (17fl oz) of strained liquid. Heat, and stir until the sugar is all dissolved.

3. Add the rum. Stir the mixture and then take it off the heat. Let it cool, and bottle in sterilised bottles.

4. To drink it: pour 3 tbsp into a tumbler and top it up with hot water.

Elderflower
Sambucus nigra

Elderflower (*Sambucus nigra*)
from Hayne: *Getreue Darstellung
und Beschreibung der in der Arzneykunde
Gebräuchlichen Gewächse*, 1809.

CAUDLE

The title of this drink comes from the Latin *calidus*, meaning 'warm'. A nourishing drink, in medieval times, caudle was given to invalids, and it survived into the 18th century as a form of refreshment offered to women recovering from childbirth. Queen Charlotte followed this custom, inviting members of the public to share cake and caudle after the births of many of her 15 children, who all spent their childhood summers at Kew.

1. Pour the green tea into a large saucepan, and place over a low heat.
2. Beat the egg yolks and mix them with the white wine, nutmeg and sugar, to taste.
3. Add the egg and wine mixture to the tea in the saucepan. Stir continually, until it is very hot. Serve in china teacups.

Serves 12

1 litre (1¾ pt) strong **green tea**

4 **egg yolks**

600ml (1pt) **white wine**

1 **nutmeg**, grated

caster sugar, to taste

Nutmeg (*Myristica fragrans*), 'Foliage, flowers and fruit of the nutmeg tree and hummingbird, Jamaica' (Plate 119) by Marianne North.

MRS BEETON'S SAVOURY BEEF TEA

Really nutritious, this beef tea is ideal for building up a person's strength if they are convalescing after an illness. Making your own beats many ready-prepared beef extracts that are available in the supermarket. The beef can always be used in a stew or pie.

Makes 600ml (1pt)

450g (1lb) **beef**

25g (1oz) **butter**

1 **clove**

2 button **onions**, or ½ a large one

1 tsp **salt**

1 litre (1¾pt) **water**

1. Cut the beef into small pieces and put the pieces in a stewing pan with the butter, clove, onions and salt. Stir the meat around over the heat for a few minutes, until it releases its juices gravy, then add the water. Let it gently simmer for 30–45 minutes, skimming off any fat.

2. Strain the beef and liquid through a sieve, and leave in a cool place until required. Reheat, the beef tea in small amounts, as desired, and serve.

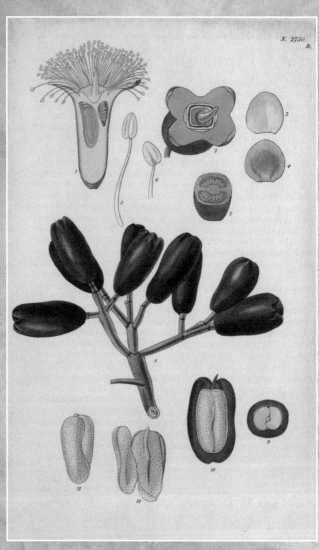

Clove (*Syzygium aromaticum*) from *Curtis's Botanical Magazine*, 1827.

EGGNOG

This is Bob Flowerdew's traditional family tonic for anyone needing something to boost them but who can't face solid food. It's also very popular in North America at Thanksgiving or Christmas. Just multiply the quantities if you want to make it for several people.

Serves 1–2

2 **eggs**, preferably fresh
1 egg cup **brandy**
1 tsp **Bourbon vanilla extract**
1 tbsp **runny honey**
300ml (½pt) **full cream milk**
ground cinnamon or **nutmeg**,
    to serve

1. Whisk the eggs, brandy and vanilla together and then pass the mixture through a fine sieve.
2. Add the honey, and whisk the mixture until all the honey has dissolved. Then whisk in the milk.
3. Chill the eggnog in the refrigerator. To serve, pour the mixture into a glass, and dust with the cinnamon or nutmeg.

Nutmeg (*Myristica fragrans*) from Bentley and Trimen: *Medicinal Plants*, 1880.

OATMEAL POSSET

First drunk in Medieval times, a posset is a hot drink made from milk that has wine or ale added to it and various spices. In the 16th century, it was usual to add lemon juice and to use cream. Traditionally, it was given to people suffering from colds or 'flu, but it makes a comforting drink for a winter's day.

The interior of a Medieval kitchen from a 16th-century facsimile of Staéffler: *Calendarium Romanum*, 1518.

1. Pour the milk into a small saucepan and add the oatmeal and salt. Heat the mixture until it is nearly boiling, then take it off the heat and allow it to stand for about 10 minutes.

2. Sieve the mixture into a clean saucepan, and add the sugar and nutmeg. Heat it again until it is almost at boiling point, stirring frequently to prevent it burning on the bottom of the saucepan. Remove the saucepan from the heat, stir in the brandy and serve.

Serves 2

600ml (1 pint) **milk**
2 tbsp **oatmeal**
¼ tsp **salt**
2 tsp **sugar**
¼ tsp **nutmeg**, freshly grated
1 tbsp **brandy** (or **whisky**, if preferred)

Nutmeg
Myristica fragrans

DRINKING GARDEN HERBS

by city gardener Sarah Heaton

What I love most about herbs is that they evoke the senses. To see a beautiful herb garden, stroke the soft felt leaf of apple mint, smell the scent released as you brush past or hear the pop of calendula as the seed is released, is to have an affinity with nature that somehow makes me feel connected. Herbs weave into my life in a charming and affirming way, whether it's drinking tea and tisanes with friends, or adding herbs to small posies or to my cooking. They are communal.

I also love herbs for their many varied and vibrant tastes, and as plants they are not too needy. They look pretty, they often taste great and some are positively medicinal. They are also easily available and easy to grow. All herbal teas are without tannin or caffeine and so much more suitable to aid digestion and promote sleep and general good health.

Kew is such an inspiration for gardeners like me. The Queen's Garden, near Kew Palace is a good place to look for new and interesting herbs as well as medicinal plants.

Growing my own herbal tea has been a tonic, too. My mother first suggested that I grew a pot of herbs when I rented a flat in Putney in my twenties. We bought a terracotta pot and several plants, including purple sage and trailing verbena, catmint, mint and rosemary, a lovely combination of purple flowers and leaves, to sit on the patio outside the kitchen and how useful this was. The mint was used more to spice up the Pimms in those days, but ever since, I have had mint near at hand to add to boiling water for mint tea or to a jug of water at meal times.

I think **mint** (*Mentha* spp.) is an especially essential herb for teas and tisanes, as there are so many varieties and it is so easy to cultivate. It can grow well in sun or shade. Probably, the best all-rounder is Moroccan mint, with its pretty, purple flower (also

'Love and scandal are the very best sweeteners of tea'.
HENRY FIELDING
(1707–1754)

The Queen's Garden at Kew.

Spearmint
Mentha spicata

edible and lovely in salads). Apple mint is another that works as well for tisanes as it does in the garden. They are all good for pollinators, too, keeping our bee community happy. The variegated versions are also attractive in gardens, in containers and on balconies. Mint has a tendency to spread so works well in a pot if you don't want it popping up everywhere. On the primary school allotment, where I work, it is everywhere, but I secretly like its wildness and unexpected appearances. We all know mint and potatoes go very well together! It is also a herb that children love to smell and touch and can easily recognise, take home and plant in their own pot or garden with great success.

The leaves of mint, especially spearmint and peppermint, infused in boiling water are good for colds, headaches, diarrhoea, heartburn, nausea and stomach-ache. Mint tea is particularly good as a digestive after a meal.

Rosemary
Rosmarinus officinalis

Rosemary (*Rosmarinus officinalis*) is another herb that I recommend for gardeners, cooks and tea drinkers. Unlike mint, which as a perennial dies back in winter, rosemary has a year-round stellar performance. It can be big or small, grown in a pot or in the ground. It has pretty blue flowers around late spring, and is delicious and energising as a fresh herbal tea as well as in cooking. A sprig in boiling water helps with headaches and insomnia. And apart from making a flavoursome hot drink, I read with amusement in *The Modern Herbal* (1974) that when the author 'lived off the land I always used it with squirrel'! It is also, of course, a traditional accompaniment to lamb.

Chamomile
Matricaria chamomilla
Chamæmelum nobile

Chamomile (*Matricaria chamomila, Chamæmelum nobile*) is soothing and a good digestive. The plant has small feathery leaves and pretty, daisy-like, white flowers. Sow the seeds in spring in a pot on your windowsill. Once they have germinated, put the pot outside in a sunny, sheltered spot. Chamomile blooms from June to October. When the plant reaches approximately 10cm (4in) tall, give it a 'hair cut'. Use the flowers and leaves to make your tea (about a teaspoon) or dry the flowers and save them to use at a later date. Infuse them in hot water for around five minutes for a comforting herbal drink.

You can grow **ginger** (*Zingiber officinale*) from fresh ginger roots bought at the supermarket by planting three fingers broken off the ginger root (or rhizome) in a container of compost. This will grow into an exotic, red-flowering plant. Dig up the root in autumn and use it for a most reviving cup of tea that will aid digestion.

Bergamot or **bee balm** (*Monarda didyma*) has vibrant, pink flowers. A member of the mint family, it contains thymol which is good for colds and sore throats. Bergamot was first used by the Oswego Native Americans in North America and after the Boston Tea Party of 1773, it was drunk by patriotic Americans. It differs from bergamot orange (*Citrus bergamia*), a fragrant citrus fruit, used to flavour Earl Grey.

Elderflower (*Sambucus nigra*), which grow in many gardens and parks, can be used to make a delicious cordial or tisane. As well as having an attractive taste, this plant promotes sleep and alleviates sore throats.

As a tea, the leaves of **angelica** (*Angelica archangelica*), which when rubbed have a lovely aroma of liquorice and aniseed, are said to help with headaches and exhaustion. This plant is architectural in stature, grows up to 1.8m/6ft tall and self-seeds freely. It was apparently named for its angelic healing qualities and the whole plant is fragrant. Angelica was traditionally used in confectionary or as a sweetmeat; its stems were candied and used as decorations and it has many other uses, such as counteracting the acidity of rhubarb while imparting its own delicate flavour. The stems are good in salads and as vegetables, while the fruits and seeds are used for both flavouring and perfumery.

The key thing for me with growing herbs for teas is the magnificent flavour they impart. A mint teabag compared to a fresh sprig of mint in a cup is a world apart in terms of taste and colour. Fresh herbs win hands down every time. Growing a vegetable garden may seem quite ambitious to some, but growing herbs really is easy. And growing herbs is an especially good introduction for children to gardening.

'Anything green that grows out of the mould Was an excellent herb to our fathers of old.'
RUDYARD KIPLING
(1865–1936)

Elderflower
Sambucus nigra

Angelica
Angelica archangelica

Tea (*Camellia sinensis*) from Köhler: *Medizinal Pflanzen*, 1883–1914.

BOOZY ICED TEAS

Balaustia.

Mala Armeniaca.

Prunus Mijrobalanus rotundus.

Apricots and plums (*Prunus* spp.) from Besler: *Hortus Eystettensis*, 1613.

GOLDEN MEADOWS

This drink was created by Ampersand Catering to celebrate 50 years of Kew at Wakehurst (Kew's garden in West Sussex). We recommend you use Taylor's of Harrogate Sencha green tea, part of a range developed in partnership with Kew experts.

Serves 1

10ml (2 tsp) **vodka**

10ml (2 tsp) **white rum**

10ml (2 tsp) **triple sec**

10ml (2 tsp) **gin**

10ml (2 tsp) **tequila**

15ml (3 tsp) **lime juice**

40ml (1½fl oz) **green tea**, cold

To serve:

ice cubes

1 **caramelised lemon slice**

1. To make the caramelised lemon boil 50ml (2fl oz) of green tea and 50g (2oz) of caster sugar until all the sugar is dissolved and it forms a thick syrup. Allow the syrup to cool slightly and then dip thin lemon slices into the caramelised mixture and leave them on a rack or sheet of greaseproof paper to cool completely.

2. Place all the listed ingredients in a cocktail shaker and shake thoroughly.

3. Put some ice cubes in a highball or sling glass and pour the mixture over the ice. Decorate with a caramelised lemon slice, and serve.

LONDON W. — Kew Gardens. — The Tea House. — LL.

SPICED APPLE SPRITZER

Spicy apple tea and a dash of chilli give a real oomph to this spritzer syrup recipe. With a little fizz as well (whether alcoholic or not), it'll perk anyone up.

Makes enough syrup for 22 portions

10 **Taylors of Harrogate Spiced Apple teabags**

1 litre (1¾ pt) boiling **water**

100g (4oz) **caster sugar**

2 **cinnamon sticks**

2 **star anise**

¼ tsp **chilli flakes**

200ml (7fl oz) **apple juice**

To serve:

sparkling wine, or
 sparkling water

crushed **ice**

1. Place the teabags in a large jug and add the boiling water. Add the sugar and spices and infuse for 2 hours.

2. To serve, pour 50ml (2fl oz) of the syrup into a glass with 120ml (4fl oz) of sparkling wine, or for a non-alcoholic version, add 50ml (2fl oz) of mineral water and 60g (2½oz) of ice.

Apple *(Malus)* from Redouté: *Choix des plus belles Fleurs et des Plus Beaux Fruits*, 1833.

PEPPERMINT MOJITO SPRITZER

Taylors of Harrogate have been developing and selling teas since 1886 and recently produced a new selection of fruit and herbal teas in partnership with the Royal Botanic Gardens, Kew. This homage to the well-known mojito cocktail is great on a hot day.

**Makes enough syrup
for 22 portions**

10 Taylors of Harrogate **peppermint leaf** teabags

1 litre (1¾ pt) boiling **water**

150g (5oz) **honey**

100ml (3½fl oz) **elderflower cordial**

juice and zest of 10 **limes**

To serve:

sparkling wine, or **sparkling water**

crushed ice

1. Place the tea bags in a large jug and pour over the boiling water. Add the other ingredients and leave the mixture to infuse for 2–4 hours.
2. To serve, pour 50ml (2fl oz) of the syrup into a glass with 120ml (4fl oz) of sparkling wine, or for a non-alcoholic version, add 50ml (2fl oz) of mineral water and 60g (2½oz) of ice.

Peppermint (*Mentha crispa*) from Plenck: *Icones Plantarum Medicinalium*, 1788–1812.

SWEET RHUBARB COCKTAIL

Tangy rhubarb fruit tea provides the base for this Taylors of Harrogate cocktail.

1. Place the teabags in a large jug and add the boiling water and leave until cool. Mix the remaining ingredients together in another jug and add the cooled tea. Leave to chill.
2. To serve, pour 40ml (1½fl oz) of the chilled rhubarb syrup into a glass. Add some crushed ice and top up with 80ml (3fl oz) of sparkling wine, or sparkling water for a non-alcoholic version.

Makes 4 portions of syrup

3 Taylors of Harrogate **Sweet Rhubarb** teabags

100ml (3½fl oz) boiling **water**

100ml (3½fl oz) **lemon juice**

50ml (2fl oz) **elderflower cordial**

2 tsp **caster sugar**

50ml (2fl oz) **ginger syrup**

1 tsp local **honey**

To serve:

sparkling wine, or **sparkling water**

crushed ice

Rhubarb
Rheum rhaponticum

SPICED FIZZY ICED TEA

Tea gives an adult edge to this refreshing recipe from Hattie Ellis, a spiced and subtle version of iced tea. She makes the point that green tea is often mistakenly infused using water that is too hot, bringing out a bitterness rather than its gentle aromatic flavours. Hattie recommends infusing the tea in a bottle of water in the fridge, an idea she picked up from tea expert Alex Fraser of East Teas. Vary the flavourings as you like, using other spices and citrus fruits.

Serves 4

3–4 tsp **honey**, to taste

juice and rind of 2 organic
   oranges

3 **cloves**

1 **cinnamon stick**

2 tsp **green tea leaves**

1 litre (1¾ pt) bottle
   of **sparkling water**
   (or still, if preferred)

1. Pour 250ml (8fl oz) of the sparkling water into a small saucepan. Stir in the honey, orange juice, the pared rind of the oranges and the spices. Bring the mixture to the boil, then turn off the heat and leave to infuse overnight.

2. Meanwhile, add the tea to the bottle of water, screw on the lid and leave to infuse in the fridge overnight.

3. The next day, taste the spice infusion. You can leave it and the tea infusion for longer if you want a stronger flavour. For a subtle flavour, leaving the infusions overnight or for up to 24 hours should be long enough. Left longer than that, the drink may become slightly tannic.

4. Strain both the fizzy water and the liquid from the spice and citrus infusion into a large jug. Taste, and add more honey for a sweeter drink. Pour the liquid into bottles with screw-top lids to keep in the fridge, or serve straight away in the jug.

Tea (*Camellia sinensis*) by unknown artist from the Company School, dating from late 18th century.

Rosa rubroides

CORDIALS AND SYRUPS

Rose (*Rosa rubeoides*) from Andrews: *Roses* vol. 2, 1828.

PEAR SYRUP

Bob Flowerdew kindly provided this delicious recipe and recommends that it is used in the same way as runny honey or maple syrup. Apparently, it is especially good over vanilla ice-cream. It is a great way to use pears that are still edible but no longer firm, or even when they are turning soft and brown inside. It can also be frozen and used throughout the year, and diluted as a squash.

Makes about 750ml (1¼pt)

1kg (2lb) **pears**, ripe but
    not rotten
water, as needed
1 **cinnamon stick**, or a 2.5cm
    (1-in) piece of **ginger root**,
    peeled, or 1 **vanilla pod**
    (optional)

1. Wash and chop the pears into roughly 2.5cm (1in) chunks, skins, pips and all.
2. Put enough water in a large saucepan to just cover the bottom, add the chopped pears and optional spices as wished.
3. Cover the saucepan with a lid and simmer the chopped pears for at least eight hours or overnight on a very low heat. The mixture should reduce to a liquid with just the skins and pips. Strain the juice through a fine sieve into a container.
4. The juice may be drunk just as it has been made or you can reduce it to a thicker syrup by gently and carefully boiling it down further. Store the syrup in the refrigerator until it is needed, or freeze as mentioned above.

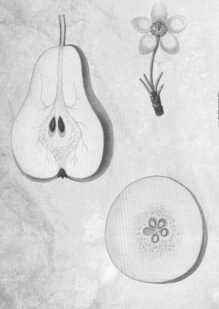

Pear (*Pyrus*) from Gallesio:
Pomona Italiana, 1820.

GINGER CORDIAL

This is a lovely cordial which can be added to many cocktails or mixed with soda water or tonic to provide a long, cooling drink. If you prefer a change, try using the same amount of a different spice, such as cardamom, cinnamon, allspice or caraway.

1. Place the ginger, or the spice of your choice in a large bowl or jug and add the gin, brandy or whisky. Allow the mixture to steep for nine days. Add sugar to taste.
2. Strain the mixture through a sieve, and bottle to use as you wish.

**Makes approximately
1 litre (2pts)**

175g(6oz) fresh **ginger**, peeled
   and cut into pieces
1 litre (1¾pt) **gin**, **brandy**
   or **whisky**
caster sugar, to taste

ZINGIBER OFFICINALE, *Roscoe.*

Ginger (*Zingiber officinale*) from Köhler: *Medizinal Pflanzen*, 1883–1914.

LIME CORDIAL

Lime cordial is particularly useful for adding to a host of recipes or for making refreshing drinks in the summer. Try using a small amount and topping up with soda water.

**Makes approximately
1 litre (1¾pt)**

1 litre (1¾pt) **lime juice**
900g (2lb) **caster sugar**
75ml (2½ fl oz) **brandy**

1. Strain the lime juice through a sieve lined with a piece of muslin or a thin tea towel, to remove any pips and bits of fruit.
2. Place the juice in a large jug add the sugar, and stir the mixture until the sugar has dissolved.
3. Add the brandy and stir well.
4. Pour the syrup into a sterilised bottle and keep in a cool place to use as desired.

Engraving of lime fruit (*C.* x *aurantifolia*) from Volkamer: *Nürnbergische Hesperides*, 1708–14.

SUGAR SYRUP

Sugar syrup is the perfect way to sweeten drinks, either hot or cold, as it mixes easily leaving no residual sugar crystals. Simply simmer equal measures of white sugar and water together until dissolved. Then bring to the boil and cook rapidly, until syrupy. Make a big batch and keep it in the fridge for up to a month.

GRAPE SYRUP

This recipe is based on one from Peter Jonas's 1818 book, *The Distiller's Guide*. It works well when diluted with sparkling water, or try adding a little bit to a trifle.

**Makes approximately
1 litre (1¾pt)**

100g (4oz) **elderflowers**
850ml (1½pt) **water**
280ml (9floz) **sherry**
1.3kg 2lb 10oz) **caster sugar**

1. Place the flowers in a large bowl or saucepan. Boil the water and pour it over the flowers. Cover the bowl or saucepan and let the mixture infuse for about 8 hours in a warm place.

2. Strain the mixture through a muslin cloth and pour the infused water into a large saucepan. Add the sherry and sugar and boil the mixture until it begins to thicken, to the point of the 'small thread' (i.e. take a small amount in a teaspoon, allow it to cool slightly, then dip a finger into the spoon, remove and touch it with your thumb; a fine thread will appear when you pull your finger and thumb apart).

3. Leave to cool and store in a sterilised bottle.

Grapes (*Vitis vinifera*) from Plenck: *Icones Plantarum Medicinalium*, 1788–1812.

RHUBARB CORDIAL

This recipe from Sarah Raven is a favourite in her home at Perch Hill. As she points out, the rhubarb is a beautiful colour — a pale opalescent pink — and particularly delicious diluted with sparkling water, with plenty of ice and a few leaves of fresh mint. A squeeze of lime is also a good addition.

Makes 1½ litres (2½pt)

2kg (4lb) **rhubarb stems**, roughly chopped

2 large **oranges**

8–10 whole **star anise**

1.2 kg (2lb 7oz) **granulated sugar**

citric acid or juice of 3 **lemons** (optional)

Rhubarb
Rheum rhaponticum

1. Put all the rhubarb into a large pan and add 1.5 litres (2½pts) of cold water; don't cover it completely with water because this dilutes the flavour of the cordial. Using a potato peeler, take four or so strips of orange zest from each orange, add this to the pan with the juice from both and add the star anise.

2. Bring the rhubarb to the boil, then turn down the heat and simmer gently, until the rhubarb is soft (it may look like a mush at this stage). Take the saucepan off the heat and allow the mixture to cool for an hour.

3. Pour the rhubarb and juice into a large jelly bag (hanging over a large bowl) and allow the juice to drip through overnight.

4. Pour the juice that has collected in the bowl into a pan and place over a low heat. Add about 600–800g (1¼–1¾lb) of the sugar, but do taste with a spoon as you go, so that you get the sweetness you want. Remember, it will get diluted with water. Stir until the sugar has dissolved.

5. You can add 2 teaspoons of citric acid at this stage if you want to store the cordial for several months, but this is not necessary if it is going to be used straightaway. The citric acid does give the cordial a good tart kick, or you can add the juice of 3 lemons for a sharper flavour. Allow the cordial to cool. Pour into sterilised bottles and store in the fridge.

Rhubarb (*Rheum rhaponticum*) from
Régnault: *La Botanique Mise à la Portée
de Tout le Monde*, 1774.

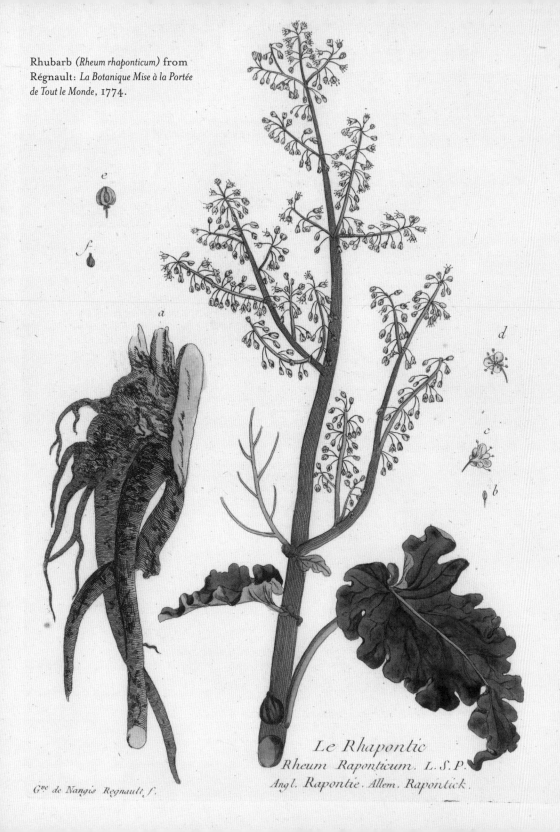

Le Rhapontic
Rheum Raponticum. L.S.P.
Angl. Rapontic. Allem. Rapontick.

G.ᵛᵉ de Nangis Regnault f.

RASPBERRY SYRUP

An unbelievably delicious syrup for pouring over desserts, adding to fruit compotes, diluting as a squash or freezing as a water ice or sorbet.

tub of **frozen raspberries** (can also be made from **tayberries** or **loganberries**), roughly same weight **sugar**

1 **egg white** (optional, for sorbet)

1. Mix the frozen fruit with sugar in a bowl and leave overnight in a cool room or refrigerator.

2. In the morning strain the fruit mixture through a muslin jelly bag to extract the juice from the pips and fruit skins. You can heat the mixture or add a little hot water before placing in the bag to help extract the juices, but this will produce a syrup of poorer flavour.

3. Pour the extracted syrup into a sterilised bottle, store in a refrigerator and use as a squash drink, diluting with water to taste. Alternatively, you can make a water ice by freezing the syrup in a plastic container, removing it every half hour or so to whisk it for about a minute, until it is frozen into a water ice. A smoother sorbet can be made by whisking in an egg white if desired.

Raspberry (*Rubus idaeus*) from Redouté: *Choix des Plus Belles Fleurs et des Plus Beaux Fruits*, 1833.

VIOLET SYRUP

This recipe is another from *The Distiller's Guide*, which offered many recipes for cordials and infusions.

1. Heat the water and pour over the flowers, cover and leave to infuse for about 8 hours in a warm place.
2. Strain the infused violet water through a muslin cloth and place in a saucepan. Add the sugar and boil the mixture until it begins to thicken, to the point of the 'small thread' (i.e. take a small amount in a teaspoon, allow to cool slightly, then dip your finger into the spoon, remove and touch it with your thumb; a fine thread will appear when you pull your finger and thumb apart).
3. Leave to cool and store in a sterilised bottle.

Makes 1 litre (1¾pt)

450g (1lb) **violet flowers**

1 litre (1¾pt) **water**

1.5kg (3½lb) **sugar**

Violets (*Viola odorata*) from Chaumeton: *Flore Médicale*, vol. 6, 1832.

PERSIAN ROSE PETAL SYRUP

Huma Qureshi's recipe for Persian Rose Petal Syrup has been passed down family generations from her great grandmother. This type of drink is very popular in hot weather because roses are said to have cooling properties. The original rose used was similar to 'Etoile de Hollande', a deep crimson, purple-pink rose. The roses were home grown, organically, and strongly perfumed, which complemented the flavour of the drink.

Makes approximately 1 bottle of syrup

1 cup (approximately 200g/7oz) perfumed **rose petals**, tightly pressed (any fragrant rose can be used)

700 ml (1¼ pt) **water**

600g (1¼lb) **caster sugar**

1. Place the rose petals in a medium-sized saucepan, cover with water and leave overnight.
2. In the morning, add the sugar to the rose petal and water mixture and stir over a low heat until the sugar is fully dissolved. Once the sugar has dissolved, increase the heat until it comes to a boil and slightly thickens. Turn off the heat and cool the mixture.
3. When the mixture is cool, test it by taking a drop of the mixture and pressing it between your finger and thumb for a thread-like consistency; as you pull your finger and thumb apart, a thread of syrup should appear.
4. Strain the mixture through a muslin cloth or sieve into a jug and refrigerate.
5. Serve the syrup with ice and add sparkling water according to taste, and decorate with small fresh rose petals.

Rose (*Rosa*) from Duhamel du Monceau: *Traité des Arbres et Arbustes*, vol. 2, 1755.

Rose *(Rosa rubiginosa)* from
Jacquin: *Flora Austriaca,* 1773.

GEORGIAN ROYAL DRINKING AT KEW

by Susanne Groom

One hundred years of summer royal occupation at Kew and nothing more than the tale of a 'bowzy' footman lying dead drunk in the street and some whisperings of the irregular habits of the young future George IV to relate ... But if the royals were not indulging in stimulating tipples during the 18th century, what were they drinking?

George II, who arrived in 1718 with Queen Caroline at Richmond Lodge, was described by Hugh Walpole as being like a horse in a treadmill, a man of such regular habits that you could set your watch by him, and he ate and drink in much the same vein, content with what he was habitually served and well within the limits of moderation. He was constantly irritated by Queen Caroline, with her passion for gardening – 'silly childish stuff' – and her excessive love of chocolate. There are numerous accounts of her breakfasting, usually on fresh fruit and soured cream, but always with a cup or two of hot chocolate, which she enjoyed drinking with her daughters, and for which the king snubbed her for being 'always stuffing'.

The young George and Caroline had taken refuge at Richmond Lodge following a family row after which they were turned out of the royal palaces, as curiously were their own son Frederick, Prince of Wales and his new wife Augusta in 1737, when they came with their baby daughter to stay in the White House, at the opposite end of what is all now Kew Gardens. Frederick was fond of parties and practical jokes, but he was no great lover of hard drink. He was seemingly happier with a single glass of choice wine and he drank water bottled from the Hotwells at Bristol and the Pouhon spring at Spa, an empty bottle of which came to light during excavations outside Kew Palace.

View of the Palace, of Her Royal Highness the Princess Dowager of Wales at Kew.

Although Frederick died aged only 44, he passed on his lack of inclination for alcohol to his eldest son, the future George III. There was nothing the new Prince of Wales liked better than a glass of cold lemon barley water, which was drunk by most of the ladies of the court, according to Queen Charlotte's dresser, the prolific diarist, Fanny Burney, who recorded the royal equerry's complaint when the King offered him his favourite tipple: 'Here, Goldsworthy, I say! he cries, will you not have a little barley water? Barley water in such a plight as that! Fine compensation for a wet jacket truly! Barley water! I never heard of such a thing in my life! Barley water after a whole day's hard hunting.'

View of the White House, the palace of HRH the Princess Dowager of Wales at Kew.

By the late 18th century, taking tea had become a daily after-dinner ritual. A regimental band – when at Kew, probably the Queen's own band – would play on the lawn, while the royal family sat indoors sipping the national beverage. Queen Charlotte liked her tea to be served in Worcester Flight china teacups and her favourite blue lily pattern design was re-named Royal Lily in her honour. The King also enjoyed his cuppa, often taking nothing more than a dish of tea and a slice or two of bread and butter after a day spent at a levée and giving a stream of audiences.

During his serious bout of illness at Kew in 1788–89, at the time diagnosed as dementia, but now thought to have been porphyria or a bipolar disorder (or possibly both) – the King's doctors habitually laced his drinks with emetics and purgatives and 'the bark', taken from the South American cinchona and in common use for the treatment of fevers. It was often added to a glass of wine to take away its bitter taste – although its most palatable and very diluted form in sweetened soda water and iced gin with a twist of lemon, was still waiting to be invented. For the household, during the King's illness, the housekeeper, Mrs Tunstall kept 'the coffee and still-room, where Betty Snoswell with her assistant attended; and night or day you were equally well served and no one was deprived of a dish of tea when required, even if not a privileged person'.

Wines regularly ordered for George III were claret and hock, Rhenish white wine and small amounts of Madeira. A caricature by Charles Williams shows George III sitting at a tea table with his Prime Minister, Henry Addington, 1st Viscount Sidmouth, at Kew Palace. It was the only occasion when the King was known to have sat down to a private meal with anyone outside his own family. Between them on the table is a bottle of Tokaji. A sweet, botrytised, Hungarian, white wine, Tokaji was the toast of Europe and drunk by Catherine of Russia, Frederick the Great and Louis XV, who christened it 'Wine of Kings and King of Wines'. It is difficult to imagine that it was much to the taste of the frugal King, but it lends another note of humour to Gillray's most famous caricature of George III, *Temperance enjoying a Frugal Meal*, in which the jug by his foot is labelled '*Aqua Regis*'.

The newspapers commented: 'Exercise, air and a light diet are the great fundamentals in the king's idea of health. His majesty feeds chiefly on vegetables and drinks but little wine.'

It is not surprising that a couple so abstemious in their own eating and drinking habits should have tried to instil the same principles into the diet of their children, whose breakfast at Kew was toast with 'milk in a basin, two thirds milk and one of tea moderately sweetened'. After dinner, the two elder princes could opt for coffee or 'one glass of any wine they chuse', but this was a special treat reserved for only two days of the week. Was it this rigid childhood regime which led the eldest son, the future George IV, into a life of excessive indulgence, ending in his miserable death in 1830? The Duke of Wellington, visiting the King towards the end of his life, expressed amazement at his breakfast, which consisted of two pigeons and three beefsteaks, accompanied by 'three parts of a bottle of Mozelle, a glass of dry champagne, two glasses of port and a glass of brandy' — but by that time, life had taken King George IV a long way from his early beginnings in the golden summers at Kew.

George III, Queen Charlotte and their Six Eldest Children. Zoffany, Royal Collection Trust.

Group of Japanese Orange Family (Aurantiaceae) Collection II, print published by the Mita Seed Raising Establishment of the Japan Agricultural Society, Tokyo, 19th year of Meiji, 1886.

FRESH SUMMER TONICS

GRANNY'S LEMONADE

This recipe comes from Jonathan Kendon's paternal grandmother's family. Grace Honess was born in 1898 in Kent and was an accomplished cook. Jonathan's parents use the recipe constantly and put their lack of colds and 'flu down to the high vitamin C content of the drink. The boiling water helps to draw out the aromatic oils from the fruit peel, while waiting for the liquid to cool before adding the lemon juice helps to preserve the vitamins. Using golden syrup gives a rich flavour to the sweetness.

Makes 1 litre (1¾pt)

juice and zest of 1 medium to
    large **lemon**
1 tbsp **golden syrup**, or
    maple syrup or **honey**
2 tsp **granulated sugar**
1 litre (1¾pt) boiling **water**
concentrated **lemon juice**

1. Peel the lemon with a potato peeler. Take care not to cut too deeply into the pith, as this will make the drink too bitter.

2. Place the peelings in the bottom of a large, heat-proof, earthenware jug. Add the golden syrup and sugar (these can be adjusted to taste). Pour in the boiling water, stir and leave to cool.

3. Squeeze the juice from the lemon and add to the jug. Stir and taste, adding a few drops of concentrated lemon juice if desired. Keep the lemonade in the fridge and consume within a few days.

Citron (*Citrus medica*) from collection of paintings by Chinese artists, probably early 19th century.

ELDERFLOWER CORDIAL

Diana Rawlinson works at Wakehurst as a member of Kew's Millennium Seed Bank support team. The countryside around Wakehurst is full of wonderful elderflower trees and she enjoys taking her dog on elderflower picking walks. This recipe was given to Diana nearly 30 years ago by friends in the New Forest and has proved hugely popular.

Makes approximately 1.4 litres (2½pts)
1 **lemon**
1 **orange**
24 **elderflower heads**
1kg (2lb) **sugar**
50g (2oz) **citric** or **tartaric acid**
1.75 litres (3pts) boiled **water**, cooled

1. Slice the fruit. Put the fruit and all the other ingredients into a large bowl or bucket and stir. Leave the mixture for 48 hours, stirring occasionally, until the sugar has dissolved.

2. Strain the contents through a muslin cloth, giving the fruit a good squeeze. Bottle, and keep in the fridge. You can also put bottles of the cordial in the freezer to store.

3. Use a small amount of the cordial and dilute to taste with water – fizzy water is really lovely with this cordial, or sparkling wine for a real treat. Try a spoonful, undiluted, poured over fruit salads or in fruit crumbles. It is also lovely to pour over lemon drizzle cake instead of lemon juice.

Elderflower (*Sambucus nigra*) from Kops': *Flora Batava*, Volume 6, 1832.

PERSIAN SWEET & SOUR MINT AND CUCUMBER DRINK

Sekanjabin is a very old drink that originates from Iran. It is made as a syrup and then diluted. The cucumber adds to the freshness of the drink. This recipe comes from Sara Fardipour, who loves to drink it on hot summer days.

Serves 6

For the Sekanjabin syrup:
240ml (8fl oz) **water**
225g (7½oz) **caster sugar**
120ml (4fl oz) **white vinegar**
a small bunch of fresh **mint**

To serve:
1.4 litres (2½pts) **water**
ice cubes
half a **cucumber**, grated

1. To make the Sekanjabin syrup: put the water and sugar in a medium-sized saucepan, and heat the mixture so that the sugar dissolves over a low heat. Then boil the mixture for 10 minutes.

2. Add the vinegar to the saucepan, turn the heat down, and simmer for approximately 20 minutes, until the syrup thickens a bit. Keep checking the consistency of the liquid during this time. When it starts to look thicker than water, it's done.

3. Take pan off heat, stir in the fresh mint and allow the mixture to cool to room temperature. Once the syrup has cooled, remove the mint.

4. To serve: mix syrup with the additional water in a large jug. Taste to see if you need to add more water. Place some ice cubes in each of the serving glasses with some grated cucumber, then pour the diluted syrup into each one.

Cucumber (*Cucumis sativus*) from Régnault: *La Botanique Mise à la Portée de Tout le Monde*, 1774.

LEMON BARLEY WATER

George III was renowned for his abstemiousness in both food and drink, as depicted in so many caricatures. His equerry was once shocked to be handed nothing more than a glass of lemon barley water at the end of a long, hard day's hunting. This, however, was the King's favourite drink and one enjoyed more especially by the ladies of the court, including the Queen's dresser, the famous diarist Fanny Burney. The lemons and oranges, normally used for flavouring barley water, were grown in the Orangery at Kew in the 18th century. In her famous cookery book of 1747, *The Art of Cookery Made Plain and Easy*, Hannah Glasse suggested adding two spoonfuls of white wine and drinking the barley water while still lukewarm.

1. Place the barley and water in a large saucepan, bring to the boil and simmer for approximately 45 minutes. Take the saucepan off the heat, and allow the barley water to cool.
2. Strain the water into a bowl or jug, and flavour with the fruit juice and lemon peel.
3. Add the sugar and pass through a sieve again into a jug. Keep covered in the fridge until required.

**Makes approximately
1 litre (1¾pt)**

1 litre (1¾pt) **water**
50–75g (2–3oz) **pearl barley**
juice of 2 **lemons** or **oranges**
peel of 1 **lemon**
4–6 tbsp **caster sugar**

The Orangery at Kew, printed by C. Hallmandel after a drawing by G. E. Papendick, 19th century.

OTTOMAN ROSE SHERBET

Roses pervade many ancient cultures. In the Ottoman Empire, rose sherbet was both a medicinal drink and a drink of hospitality served at banquets. Sherbets can be flavoured with numerous fruits, flowers and spices.

Makes approximately 1.5 litres (2½ pt)

1.5 litres (2½ pt) **water**
15g (½oz) dried **rose petals***
85g (3½oz) **caster sugar**
juice of ½ **lemon**

1. Pour the water into a large saucepan with a well fitting lid and bring it to the boil.
2. Add the rose petals, and stir to mix them thoroughly. Then turn off the heat, and cover the saucepan with the lid. Leave the water to cool to room temperature with the lid on.
3. Once the water is cool, strain it, retaining the liquid and discarding the petals. Add the sugar and lemon juice, and stir.
4. Classically, rose sherbet is served chilled. It can also be served warm as an aromatic tea. Alternatively shaken with ice and rum and strained into a glass it makes an excellent rose daiquiri.

* If buying dried rose petals for cooking or making drinks, make sure they are food-grade quality. Rose petals supplied for wedding confetti or potpourri may have been treated with chemicals while growing that render them unsuitable for consumption. When drying your own rose petals, dark pink or red ones give the best colour to drinks. Pick fragrant and well-petalled roses for the most flavour and for speed. Good examples include Rosa 'Roseraie de l'Hay', Provence roses (*Rosa* x *centifolia*) or Damask roses (*Rosa* x *damascena*).

The Moss Provence Rose by Ehret, from Trew: *Hortus Nittidissimus*, 1750.

ROSE SHERBET is a drink that can span a lifetime. In Turkey, rose sherbet is served at significant occasions, starting as the drink offered to those who visit a baby 40 days after its birth. It is also drunk on the occasions of circumcisions, engagements, weddings and wakes. Even before electric refrigeration, sherbet was a refreshing beverage for hot summer days as it was served over shaved ice. Spring snow was harvested from hills, stored in icehouses and then sold in the summer by karci (snow dealers).

SANGUINELLA SOUR

Non-alcoholic, bright and refreshing, this is a lovely citrus drink that is equally delicious made from a mixture of regular orange juice and lemons. For an unusual background flavour, add a handful of pineapple mint to the jug when in season.

1. Place the ice in a tall jug and pour over the blood orange juice. Add the lime juice and tonic water, and stir briefly to mix.
2. Serve the cocktail in tall glasses and add a dash of the angostura orange bitters before serving.

Makes 1 litre (1¾ pt)

4 handfuls of **crushed ice**
400ml (14fl oz) freshly squeezed
    blood orange juice
juice of 4 large **limes**
600ml (1pt) **tonic water**
angostura orange bitters

Orange (*Citrus x aurantium*) from Poiteau: *Pomologie Française*, 1846.

WHEY

Although called 'healing water' by the ancient Greek physicians, whey has often been considered as nothing more than a by-product of cheese-making. In the mid 18th century, however, it gained popularity as a health-giving drink in the fashionable spas of Europe. Sellers of curds and whey were a common sight in the streets of 18th century London. It is a drink which is soothing to the digestion, and which was also believed to be beneficial for gout. John Wesley maintained that it could cure nosebleeds.

Makes 1 litre (1¾ pt)

1 litre (1¾ pt) **milk**

1 tbsp **lemon juice**,
     or **verjuice**

1. Pour the milk into a medium-sized saucepan and heat. Stir the milk constantly and when it is almost rising to the boil (but not yet boiling), take it off the heat and add the lemon juice or verjuice, and continue stirring until the milk curdles.
2. Strain the whey through a fine muslin or cheese cloth, or even a clean tea towel, into a jug or bowl, and keep it covered in the fridge.
3. Whey can be drunk immediately warm or cold. It can also be left to ferment further, making it a sparkling drink. The curds can be sweetened and eaten like cream with seasonal soft fruit, or with a pinch of salt and some herbs to taste, you can enjoy it as a delicious soft cheese.

Engraving of lemon fruit from Johann Christoph Volkamer's *Nürnbergische Hesperides*, 1708–14.

With so many royal children at Kew during the summer months to cater for and no refrigeration, whey provided a refreshing and nutritious drink in plentiful supply for them during play in the gardens, or perhaps while sitting quietly on their tuffets.

MRS BEETON'S GINGER BEER

Ginger beer became very popular in Britain from the mid 18th century onwards when brewing it began in Yorkshire. It then spread around the world including North America. Mrs Beeton's household obviously drank a lot of it, given the quantities of this recipe, but you can reduce this to make a smaller amount as you desire.

1. Peel the lemons, squeeze the juice, strain it and put the peel and juice into a large saucepan with the ginger, cream of tartar and loaf sugar.

2. Add the boiling water, and let it stand until just warm. Then add the yeast, which should be thick and perfectly fresh. Stir the pan well, and leave the contents in a warm room overnight, covering the pan with a cloth.

3. Next day, skim off the yeast, and pour the liquid into another container, leaving the sediment. Bottle immediately (in sterilised bottles), and cork firmly or use airtight stoppers. It's advisable to leave a small gap between the beer and the top of each bottle, so that the gases that form have somewhere to sit. Leave the beer for three days before drinking. If you prefer a less sweet beer, reduce the amount of sugar.

Makes 48 bottles

peel and juice of 2 **lemons**
40g (1½oz) bruised **ginger**
25g (1oz) **cream of tartar**
1.1kg (2¼lb) **loaf** or **granulated sugar**
13.5 litres (3 gallons) boiling **water**
2 large tbsp thick and fresh **brewer's yeast**

Manufacture of sugar at Katipo, near Tete, Mozambique, by Thomas Baines, 1859.

OMA'S WHITTENHAM CIDER

A hearty, non-alcoholic recipe for cider and a great way to use up windfall apples of any variety, whether eating or cooking types.

**Makes approximately
7 litres (1½ gallons)**

1.5kg (3lb) **apples** (eating
   or cooking, or a mixture
   of both)

7 litres (12 pt) **water**

1kg (2lb) granulated **sugar**

juice and zest of 3 **lemons**

1. Wash the apples, cut them into quarters and blitz them in a food processor, including the core and pips.

2. Place the apples in a large pan or a clean bucket and add the water. Cover the pan, and leave it in cool place for a week, stirring each night and morning.

3. At the end of the week, strain off the liquid carefully (through a muslin or thin tea towel), and discard the apple. Add the sugar and the juice and zest of the lemons to the liquid. Leave the mixture for 24 hours.

4. After 24 hours, strain the liquid again and bottle it in clean plastic or glass bottles with tight lids. (Don't fill the bottles right up, but allow about 10cm (4in) space at the neck to give the gas that develops somewhere to sit.) Store in a cool, dark place.

5. The cider can be drunk after 2 weeks, but it will improve very much if kept for a couple of months. Beware: it can be highly explosive!

Apple (*Malus*) from Poiteau: *Pomologie Française*, 1846.

HUNTE'S GINGER LEMONADE

This recipe comes from Kew volunteer Mike Beament, courtesy of Anthony Hunte, the plantsman and owner of Hunte's Gardens, which are 'some of the most beautiful gardens in Barbados'. The quantities were originally provided in cup measurements, so they have also been reproduced here, and the metric and imperial measurements are an approximation.

Mix all the ingredients in a large jug or container and chill in the refrigerator. Use as required.

Makes approximately 6 pints

700ml (1¼ pt) (3 cups) **lemon or lime juice**

450ml (16fl oz) (2 cups) **simple cane syrup**

450ml (16fl oz) (2 cups) **ginger syrup***

2 litres (3½ pt) (8½ cups) **water**

A dash of **angostura bitters**

Hunte's Gardens, Barbados.

*ginger syrup

1. Bring the sugar and water to a boil in a saucepan over medium-high heat, stirring to dissolve sugar.
2. Add the ginger and heat to boiling point. Continue to boil until the liquid quantity has reduced by half. Remove from heat, leave to steep for 30 minutes. Pour the syrup through a fine sieve to remove the ginger, place in a sterilised bottle, cool and refrigerate. The syrup will keep for one month.

Makes about 500ml

500g (1lb) **sugar**

1 litre (1¾pt) **water**

200g (7oz) **fresh ginger**, peeled and cut into very thin slices

Ginger
Zingiber officinale

Banana (*Musa*) from Cowell:
The Curious and Profitable Gardener, 1730.

The Flower, fruit,
& plant, of the
Bonanas.

SMOOTHIES

The Bonanas Flower in full proportion

The Fruit of the Bonanas in Proportion.

The Triangular Torch Thistle.

BASIC FRUIT SMOOTHIE

If you keep a bowl of fruit and any of them are becoming too soft, smoothies are an ideal way of using them up. So they are always different and exciting; don't be afraid to experiment. Here's Sarah Heaton's standard recipe and method.

Serves 3–4

1 **kiwi***, peeled

1 **banana** (the browner the skin the better)

3 tbsp **oats**

1 tsp of **sugar** or **honey**

a handful of **frozen redcurrants**

125ml (4fl oz) **apple** or **orange juice**

100g (4oz) **plain yogurt**

150–300 ml (¼–½pt) **milk**

a sprig of **mint**

1. Put all the ingredients and half the milk in a blender and blitz for three minutes.
2. Add more milk as desired to make the mixture more liquid or leave it thick, to eat with a teaspoon.
* This can be exchanged for strawberries, raspberries or any other favourite fruit that you may have.

BELOW: Apple (*Malus*) from Nicholson: *The Illustrated Dictionary of Gardening*, 1888.

RIGHT: Banana (*Musa paradisiaca*) by Ehret from Trew: *Plantae selectae*, vol. 2, 1751.

SMOOTHIE VARIATIONS

BANANA AND PEAR

The use of chilled pears gives a delicious light
taste to the overall combination of fruit.

Serves 3–4

2 ripe **pears**

1 **lemon**, squeezed

125ml (4fl oz) **orange juice**

2 ripe **bananas**, peeled

100g (4oz) **plain yogurt**

1 tsp ground **cinnamon**

milk or **orange juice**, if needed

Pear *(Pyrus)* from Poiteau:
Pomologie Française, 1846.

Peel the pears and cut them into quarters. Put them on the baking tray and place
the tray in the freezer for at least 20 minutes, then blend all the ingredients until
smooth. Add milk or orange juice to reach the desired consistency.

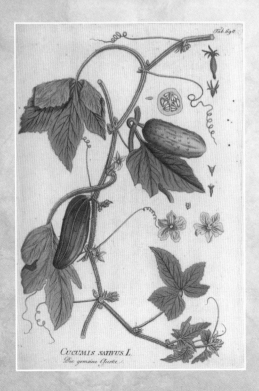

Cucumis sativus L.
Die gemeine Gurke.

COURGETTE AND CUCUMBER

Great for the summer; the combination
is very refreshing.

Serves 3

1 **courgette**, cooked and cooled

½ **cucumber**, peeled and chopped

a handful of **mint**

100g (4oz) **plain yogurt**

milk, if needed

Place all the ingredients, except the milk in a
blender and blend until smooth. Add milk to
reach the desired consistency.

Cucumber *(Cucumis sativus)* from Plenck:
Icones Plantarum Medicinalium, 1788–1812.

APRICOT AND ALMOND

A classic combination makes this a tasty treat for breakfast or a mid-morning snack.

Serves 2

5 ripe **apricots** or canned **apricots**
50g (2oz) **flaked almonds**
100g (4oz) **plain yogurt**
300ml (½pt) **milk**
ice cubes

Apricot and plum (*Prunus* spp.) from Twining: *Illustrations of the Natural Orders of Plants*, 1849-55.

PEACHES AND CREAM

Redolent of a warm summer afternoon in the garden, this is the perfect way to cool down.

Serves 2

1 tin of **peaches** in natural juice
150ml (¼pt) **double cream**
ice cube

Peach (*Prunus persica*) from Poiteau: *Pomologie Française*, 1846.

AVOCADO

Full of healthy goodness, the ripe avocado gives a lovely smooth texture, perked up by the tangy juices of the lemon and lime. Make a sweet or savoury version as you prefer.

Serves 2

1 ripe **avocado**, skinned and stoned
juice of half a **lemon**
juice of half a **lime**
300ml (½pt) **milk**
1 tsp **caster sugar** or a pinch of **salt**
ice cubes

Avocado (*Persea americana*) from Jacquin: *Selectarum Stirpium Americanarum Historia*, 1780-1781.

BLUEBERRY VITALITY SMOOTHIE

A great booster for any gym enthusiast after a workout; hugely nutritious and good for rebuilding muscle.

Serves 1

25g (1oz) **blueberries**, frozen
1 sliced **banana**
200ml (7fl oz) **milk**
25g (1oz) **whey protein** (chocolate or the flavour of your choice)

Blueberry (*Vaccinium*) from Plenck: *Icones Plantarum Medicinalium*, 1788–1812.

PEANUT BUTTER AND BANANA

A favourite of Antony Berry's girlfriend, who loves peanut butter, but was fed up of having it just on bread.

Serves 1

1 sliced **banana**

a pinch of ground **cinnamon**

1 large tbsp smooth **peanut butter**

250ml (8fl oz) **milk**

Peanut (*Arachis hypogaea*) from Köhler: *Medizinal Pflanzen,* 1883–1914.

JUS ALPOKAT

Kew botanist Tim Utteridge, explains the origins of this avocado-based drink: 'In Timor, at the night market (Pasir Panjang, Kupang), I watched the fruit juice stall and this was their recipe. The juice was a bit weak, either because the fruit was too small and there was too much ice, or the fruit was picked too early and not ripe enough to have any great flavour. Experiment with good ripe fruit and the amount of ice to get it just right.'

1. Place all the ingredients, except the chocolate condensed milk, into a blender and process until very smooth. This can take a while.
2. Swirl the chocolate condensed milk around the inside of the serving glass. Pour the mixture into the glass, and serve.
* make this by blending 50g (2oz) of melted, dark, unsweetened chocolate into a 400ml (14oz) tin sweetened condensed milk.

Serves 1

1 small, ripe **avocado**
2 large tbsp **condensed milk**
2–3 tbsp **caster sugar**
ice, of an equivalent volume to the avocado
2 tbsp **chocolate condensed milk***

The GIS research team from the Royal Botanic Gardens, Kew, drinking Jus Alpokat during a field trip to the Harapan rainforest in Sumatra, Indonesia.

MAKING CIDER

by Bob Flowerdew

My family have been making cider for many generations. Here in East Anglia, we don't use varieties of cider apples, but a mixture of dessert and culinary apples. Thus, our ciders are more like a white wine and do not much resemble West Country scrumpy or commercial ciders, or 'sui-ciders' as we call them.

The method remains the same, though it is easier to produce consistent quality now the old wooden crushers and presses have been replaced. These were huge, requiring big batches and much labour, mostly to keep everything clean. Modern stainless steel and plastic equipment is more conducive to processing smaller, more manageable batches and is much easier to clean. Further improvement has also come from better, more reliable yeasts.

Another slight change is that we now drink much more as juice. The first stage in cider making is to extract clean, fresh apple juice. We used to drink this nectar only on the days we made it because it fermented if kept. Now, we freeze the best juice in plastic bottles to quaff during the rest of the year. It's far better than any commercial juice, though it still ferments within a few days of de-frosting.

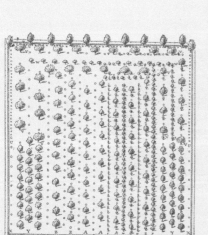

To make cider, you will need:

Equipment

Buckets, to collect and wash the apples

1–2 **sharp knives**

1 large stainless-steel or food-grade **bowl** or **bucket**, to hold the cut pieces

2 stainless-steel or glass **bowls**, to collect the juice

Sieve

Funnel

Apple crusher, bought or home made. This reduces apples to a 'bitty' pulp. Too chunky and it won't give up all its juice; too slurry-like and it will be hard to stop it 'toothpasting' out. I have known some people who have put cleaned apples in heavy duty plastic bags and driven the car over them!

Apple press, bought or home made. Slatted-sided grape presses work really well with 'bitty' pulp, but they need lining with a nylon straining bag or a pillow case if the crusher produces more slurry-like pulp. Older presses used tiers of wooden platters alternating with cotton-wrapped wads of pulp, which worked well with slurry pulps, but were hard to keep clean. A huge advantage with modern equipment is that the juice is less prone to ferment 'naturally' because of undesirable yeasts, thus keeping

longer if required as juice and more importantly allowing the white wine yeasts to do a better job.

Food-grade **fermenting vat**, or several, preferably stainless steel or glass, with a fermentation lock, or wad of cotton wool.

Hydrometer, to test specific gravity. This is an inexpensive fishing-float-like gadget that records how strongly alcoholic your juice will become.

Bottles and corks, for sparkling wine, you need pressure-safe bottles with suitable closures, such as old champagne bottles, or flip-top beer bottles, such as old Grolsch bottles, or simply plastic lemonade bottles.

Ingredients

apples, approximately two parts culinary, such as bramley's seedling – though any cooking apple will serve – and one part dessert apples, preferably mid-season, though again any will do

yeast, as used for white wine

finings, or **egg whites**, to clear cloudy ferments

caster sugar, approximately 450–900g (1–2lb) per gallon for stronger, more wine-like, cider

How to make cider:

1. Start by preparing the yeast. Following the instructions on the packet, add the yeast to some warm water and sugar in a bottle and stop the bottle up with cotton wool.

2. Wash the apples. If they are dirty, use a little detergent, then rinse them twice rinse and drain.

3. Quarter the apples, leaving the skins and seeds, but remove any bruised areas, infestations or damaged areas. DO NOT include anything that you would not eat.

4. Place the apple quarters in the crusher as soon as there's enough to process. The pulp can be collected in another bowl and transferred to the press and gently tamped down. Once the press is full, fit the top on and begin pressing.

5. Pressure should be applied slowly until the juice runs freely. Then ease off the pressing to allow the pulp to expand, and then squeeze it again, increasing the pressure slightly. Repeat this process until the press reaches its limit. Do not rush it because too much sudden pressure results in less juice and may damage the press.

6. Collect the juice in a bowl, then pass it through a fine sieve and funnel it into the fermentation vat, or straight into plastic bottles for freezing as juice. Measure some of each run with the hydrometer to tell how much sugar to add later.

7. Add the yeast that you had prepared earlier to the juice in the vat, making sure that the vat is no more than four fifths full to allow for expansion. Fit the air lock or cotton wool wad to stop up the vat to exclude flies, dust and to let out gas.

8. Store the vat somewhere that is slightly warmer than the ambient outdoor autumn temperature. If it is too warm, the flavour won't be good; too cold, and fermentation will be too slow.

9. Once the initial fermentation slows down (it will usually take between a fortnight and a month), rack the liquid off the lees, the sediment in the bottom, into a temporary clean container. Then wash out the vat, and pour the fermenting liquid back in. Add sugar to bring the liquid up to the required strength. Do this slowly, or the whole lot will froth up and decamp! The hydrometer will be accompanied by instructions advising how much sugar is needed: apple juice will read about 1020–1040, which will make a weak cider. Adding sugar makes it stronger and it will keep better. If you push it above 1080–1090, it will make the cider too strong and the flavour won't be right. Most apple juice will require about 450g/1lb sugar per gallon to bring it up to the strength of dry white wine. Do not exceed this without contemplating vicious hangovers!

10. Allow the cider to continue fermenting until it ceases completely, which should take approximately 1–3 months. If you are using a plastic fermentation vat, the cider may never clear naturally unless you add finings or egg whites to settle the particles. Metal or glass vessels usually clear unaided as fermentation stops.

11. If you do use finings of some sort, once the cider has cleared, transfer it off the lees once more, either into suitable storage vats or bottles, so that the taste does not become impaired.

12. What you have now is a still, dry, white cider, which will be drinkable within the year, but best before three or so have passed. Or, turn the fresh cider into a sparkling variety by bottling it in pressure-safe bottles, adding a teaspoonful of sugar to each before sealing. This develops into a sparkling wine with a small amount of sediment. To serve, decant the wine into a jug without disturbing any sediment.

Apple (Malus) from Duhamel du Monceau: *Traité des Arbres et Arbustes*, vol. 2, 1755.

Hop (*Humulus lupulus*)
from Bigelow: *American
Medical Botany*, 1820.

CIDERS, BEERS AND WINES

Hop (*Humulus lupulus*) from Miller: *Illustratio Systematis Sexualis Linnaei*, 1804.

CIDER NECTAR

Adapted from a recipe in Jerry Thomas's *Bartender's Guide* of 1862, this is cider with a bit of a kick. Great at any time of the year, the fruity flavours combine well to lift the spirits.

Serves 6

1 litre (1¾ pt) **cider**
1 litre bottle **soda water**
50ml (2 fl oz) **sherry**
50ml (2 fl oz) **brandy**
juice of half a **lemon** and
    peel of one quarter
sugar and **nutmeg**. to taste
pineapple extract, to taste
a sprig of **verbena**
crushed ice, to serve

1. Place all the ingredients except the sugar, nutmeg and pineapple extract in a large jug or glass bowl. Stir thoroughly and strain into a clean jug.
2. Add the sugar, nutmeg and pineapple extract, as desired, to taste. Then add some crushed ice. Pour into high ball glasses and serve.

Apple (*Malus*) from Poiteau:
Pomologie Française, 1846.

MEADER

Megan Gimber, who works in the Kew Herbarium, offers a tasty cross between mead and cider. It is not as sweet as mead because all the sugars ferment, leaving a semi-dry cider, with floral notes from the honey. Try a local honey if it's available, because it is less likely to have been filtered and processed and so should still contain pollen. Experiment with the ratios (2:1 in this instance) to suit your taste.

1. Pour the apple juice into a one-gallon demijohn (it must have an airtight lock). It should be about two thirds full. It is best to make your own apple juice either by using a cider press or a juicer. Use a mix of apples, and include some cooking apples to give more flavour.
2. Top the demijohn up with the honey water. Seal the demijohn with an airlock and leave it in a cool, dark place to ferment for 2 months.
3. After two months, strain the liquid off the sediment and put into a fresh, clean demijohn and leave for another 6 months. It will then be ready to drink or it can be bottled.

Makes approximately 4.5 litres (1 gallon)

3 litres (5¼ pt) **apple juice**
1.5 litres (2½ pt) **honey water***

*To make the honey water: dissolve the contents of two 340g (12oz) jars of honey in enough water to make the mixture up to 1.5 litres (2½ pt)

Apple (*Malus*) from Bull: *The Herefordshire Pomona*, 1876-85.

RHUBARB AND ELDERFLOWER 'CHAMPAGNE'

According to Megan Gimber, who kindly provided this recipe, the 'champagne' will vary in taste from sweet to dry, depending on when fermentation is stopped. You can use tough, old rhubarb, but make sure you harvest the elderflowers in the morning of a bright sunny day. If you pick them later than 11.00 am, the flowers get a bit warm and start smelling musty.

Makes approximately 4.5 litres (1 gallon)

1.4kg (3lb) **rhubarb**, chopped
1.4kg (3lb) **caster sugar**
5–10 **elderflower heads**
1 sachet **brewer's yeast**

1. Place the rhubarb and sugar in a large bowl. Cover it and leave it overnight for the sugar to suck all the juice out of the rhubarb.

2. The following day, pour the juice into a demijohn (which should have an airlock). To extract any remaining flavour, boil some water and pour it over the old rhubarb pieces. Leave the water to cool down a bit, then add the elderflower heads and allow the mixture to infuse overnight.

3. Strain the elderflower and rhubarb water, and top the demijohn up with this liquid. Add a sachet of brewer's yeast, and further water to fill the demijohn up to the neck if needed.

4. Seal the demijohn with an airlock and leave the champagne to ferment for 1 month. After a month, bottle the liquid (being careful to avoid the sediment at the bottom) into old champagne bottles, seal with plastic corks and attach a wire cage. The 'champagne' can be drunk after 4 months, but will last over a year. The end result should be naturally fizzy, both fruity and floral, with a wonderful summery aroma of elderflower. It is perfect when served chilled.

Elderflower (*Sambucus nigra*) from Woodville, Hooker & Spratt: *Medical Botany*, 1832.

BEETROOT WINE

There has been a revival of interest in beetroot over the last few years and this wine is based on an old 18th century recipe. You will need to be patient because it takes at least six months before it is ready to drink, but it is a lovely way to use up a glut of beetroot and the beetroot themselves can be used in numerous ways once cooked.

1. Wash the beetroot thoroughly, but don't peel them. Cut them into thin slices.

2. Place the beetroot and the water in a large saucepan or stockpot and bring the water to the boil. Simmer the beetroot for 30–40 minutes until it is tender (you can test it with a knife, which should go in easily).

3. Strain the liquid into a large bowl, big enough to hold the 6–8 litres (12 pt) of water. Keep the beetroot to use in salads. Then pour the water back into the saucepan and add the sugar, cloves and oranges. Heat the mixture over a low heat, stirring constantly to help dissolve the sugar, and boil it gently for 15 minutes.

4. Strain the liquid into the bowl once more and leave it to cool to about 20°C (70°F). Add the yeast and stir once. Cover the bowl with a clean cloth and leave the mixture for three days, but stir it each day.

5. After three days, strain the liquid once more into a large demijohn (sufficient to hold 4.5 litres/1 gallon). The liquid should come up to the bottom of the neck of the jar. Put an airtight lid on the demijohn and leave until fermentation stops. If a sediment (lees) forms in the bottom of the jar, siphon the wine off into a clean demijohn. *

6. Once fermentation has stopped, bottle the wine, and leave for a minimum of 6 months before drinking.

*this is called 'racking'

Makes 4.5 litres (1 gallon)

1.4kg (3lb) uncooked **beetroot**

6–8 litres (10-12 pt) **water**

1.4kg (3lb) **granulated sugar**

6 **cloves**

3 **oranges**, sliced

15g (½oz) **brewer's yeast**

Beetroot (*Beta vulgaris*) from Mattioli: *Commentaries in six volumes on De Materia Medica of the Physician Dioscorides of Anazarba*, 1559-1660.

MRS BEETON'S GOOSEBERRY WINE

Ideal for using up gooseberries when they ripen in June and July, this wine takes up to a year to prepare and mature. In her original instructions, Mrs Beeton states that this wine's 'briskness depends more upon the time of bottling than upon the unripe state of the fruit, for effervescing wine can be made from fruit that is ripe as well as that which is unripe. The fruit should be selected when it has near attained its full growth.'

**Makes approximately
4.8 litres (1 gallon)**

4.8 litres (8 pt) warm **water**
3kg (6lb) **gooseberries**
1.5kg (3lb) **granulated sugar**
brandy, to swill the cask
isinglass (optional)

1. Check over the gooseberries and discard any that are damaged or decayed. Do not include any stalk ends. Place the gooseberries
in a large bowl or stockpot and crush them slightly.

2. Pour over the water and then squeeze and stir the gooseberriesby hand until the pulp is removed from the skins and seeds. Cover the bowl or pan with a clean cloth and leave it for 24 hours.

3. Strain the liquid through a coarse cloth (a tea towel is fine), and squeeze as much liquid out as you can into another large stockpot. Add the sugar, and stir well until dissolved. Place the pot in a warm area, cover and leave it for 1–2 days until it has fermented.

4. Draw off the liquid into a clean container (a demijohn is ideal), placed at an angle so that any scum that develops can be skimmed off, but the liquid reserved. When the active fermentation has finished, the container can be stood upright.

5. Put a stopper loosely on the container and leave it for a few more days until the fermentation is almost stopped (any hissing noises that might have come from the container will stop). At this point, drive the stopper in firmly.

6. Leave the wine for 4–5 months (Mrs Beeton talks of the next stage taking place in November or December), and then rack it, (to discard any sediment) into a clean container that has been swilled with brandy.

7. One month later, if the wine is clear, it is ready to bottle. If not, fine the wine using a small amount of isinglass (follow the manufacturer's instructions regarding quantities, depending on how much wine you are making) to clarify it. Leave the wine for a further 2–3 months.

8. Once the wine is ready, you can bottle it. Old champagne bottles are good, but it will be necessary to wire, or tie down the corks. Leave the bottles in a cool, dark place for at least a couple of months, or until you are ready to use them. Serve chilled.

Gooseberry
(*Ribes uva-crispa*)
from Brookshaw:
Pomona Britannica,
1812.

NETTLE BEER

During the 18th century, beer was brewed for the royal household and workers on the estate at Kew in a small brew house situated near the kitchens, which served the royal residence, the White House. The beer would have been for everyday drinking and probably quite low in alcohol — though this could vary according to the amount of sugar in the mixture when it was still fermenting. On one occasion, Queen Charlotte complained that her coachman was too drunk to perform his duties, but this seems to have been an isolated incident. For those without their own brew house, a simpler summer-time version is this nettle beer.

Makes approximately
4.8 litres (1 gallon)

4.8 litres (8 pt) **water**

1kg (2lb) tips of young **nettles**, freshly gathered

peel and juice of 2 **lemons**

600g (1lb) **demerara sugar**

25g (1oz) **cream of tartar**

1 tsp **dried yeast**

The White House at Kew from the Leslie Paton Collection, Orleans House Gallery.

1. Pour the water into a large saucepan and add the nettles and lemon peel. Bring to the boil and simmer for 20 minutes.

2. Place the sugar and cream of tartar in a large bowl or heatproof jug, and strain the hot liquid onto them. Stir the mixture well, and leave to cool slightly.

3. When it has cooled to blood temperature, stir in the lemon juice and yeast and keep the mixture covered in a warm place for three days, then in a cooler room for a further two days.

4. After two days, you can bottle the beer (use sterilised bottles), but it may still be fermenting, so be sure to use strong bottles, lightly corked. The beer will be ready to drink after one week.

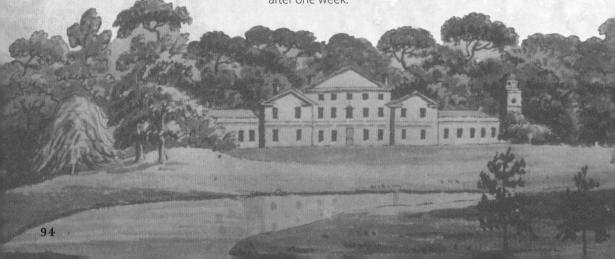

A GINSTITUTION:

A WHISTLE-STOP SNAPSHOT OF GIN IN ENGLAND
by Sophie Missing

Gin is as quintessentially British as a nice cup of tea, and London dry gin is as synonymous with the capital as double-decker buses, Big Ben, or Beefeaters. Can a spirit be more manifestly British than Beefeater Gin? I think not. Gin doesn't just have one phrase in Cockney rhyming slang; it has five. We've all heard it referred to as mother's ruin, but should you want to be a bit more niche, try ordering a needle and pin, a nose and chin, a Vera Lynn, or an Anne Boleyn next time you're at the bar, and see how you get on.

The association hasn't always been a happy one. For many years, the words 'gin' and 'poverty' were almost interchangeable; it's a hang-up from this that still makes us think of gin as a maudlin drink, prone to causing bouts of weeping or anger. In 1839, the historian Thomas Carlyle described it as 'liquid madness sold at tenpence the quartem'. Not exactly what you want from a 6.00 pm snifter. In fact, it wasn't until the advent of cocktails in the 1920s and '30s that gin became associated with the 'bright young things', which made it acceptable as a drink for the upper rungs of society. These days, thanks to a new wave of distilleries, a 'G&T' is as at home being wheeled out on the lawn of a country manor, as it is being doled out at the local boozer, or served with a flourish in a frosty martini at the Savoy.

As with so many things that become strongly associated with a place, if you go back far enough, gin isn't really British at all. Though the origins of the drink are murky, we know that the name itself comes from the French for juniper, *genièvre*, which was adopted by the Dutch and evolved to become 'genever' — a spirit that had been steeped with juniper berries and spices to take the rough edge off the taste. The resulting concoction

'Asked what you'd like to drink, say simply, "Gin, please."'
KINGSLEY AMIS,
Everyday Drinking

Juniper
Juniperus communis

Nutmeg
Myristica fragrans

Lemon
Citrus x *limon*

Star anise
Illicium verum

Orange
Citrus x *aurantium*

was sold in pharmacies and considered to help alleviate the symptoms of gout and other ailments. Perhaps unsurprisingly, this crude medicine became popular, especially with British soldiers who picked up a taste for it in the Low Countries during the Thirty Years' War. Have you ever wondered where the phrase 'Dutch courage' came from? British soldiers drinking genever is the (alleged) answer. But it wasn't until the Dutch William of Orange – William III – was crowned King of England in 1689 that gin really hit the big time.

The distillation of gin was actively encouraged during William's reign, with the law allowing anyone to make spirits out of grains if they posted a notice and waited the specified ten days. Low grain prices made it easy to make cheap (if not quality) gin – with disastrous results. We may think of binge drinking as a modern phenomenon, but it was alive and well in the 17th century with rotgut gin (an early version of the bathtub gin that would become so famous during Prohibition in the United States). The Gin Act of 1729 – and the seven following acts passed – attempted to control the situation by raising taxes on spirits and implementing new licensing laws. This met with little success, simply encouraging black market production and dealing. What had been a craze became an epidemic, and by 1751, there were as many as 17,000 'private gin shops' in London (the population at the time was 600,000). The out of control guzzling of gin was blamed for the increase in crime, immorality, disease – and, with a visibly increasing mortality rate, death. William Hogarth's famous etching Gin Lane sums up the horror of the situation, with the horribly leering, drunken mother at the image's centre surrounded by poverty and misery. Interestingly, the accompanying Hogarth drawing, Beer Street, shows the acceptable face of drinking: it's gin, not alcohol, that is insidiously evil.

While Georgian gin shops had been basic, getting the job of serious drinking done with little glamour, the gin palaces that started to appear in the late 1820s were anything but. Dickens described them in 1836, contrasting their elaborate, opulent appearance with 'the drunken besotted men, and wretched broken-down miserable women' who haunted them. Though Dickens wanted social reform, he was far from being in favour of teetotalism, being very partial to a gin punch himself. Changing the habits of a gin-soaked nation was a slow process, but following a parliamentary committee investigating the causes of drunkenness, and the social innovations of the Victorian era, the thrall of gin palaces began to wane and many were converted into that other very British institution – the pub.

Nutmeg
Myristica fragrans

The years that followed brought the development of the more delicate, botanical London dry gin and a vogue for many different gin-based drinks. Interestingly, many of the most enduring of these have medicinal aspects, bringing gin right back to where it started. From the anti-malarial gin and tonic, with quinine produced from cinchona seeds originating from the Royal Botanic Gardens, Kew, to pink gin, i.e. gin and bitters, supposedly a cure for seasickness, and the scurvy-bashing gimlet, beloved of sailors (in the words of Raymond Chandler, 'a real gimlet is half gin and half Rose's Lime Juice and nothing else'.

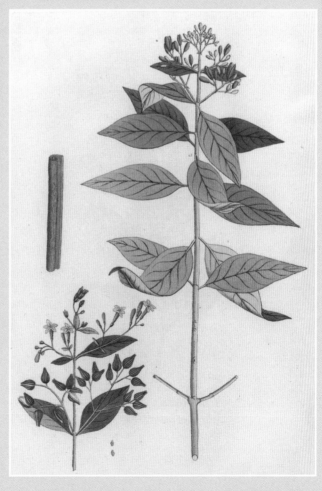

Cinchona (*Cinchona officinalis*)
from Plenck: *Icones Plantarum Medicinalium*, 1788–1812.

W.Müller n.d.Nat

Juniper (*Juniperus communis*) from Köhler: *Medizinal Pflanzen*, vol. I, 1887

BOTANICAL COCKTAILS

Elderberries *(Sambucus nigra)* from Köhler: *Medizinal Pflanzen*, 1883–1914.

SPICED TONIC

The warm, plummy and marzipan top notes of the sloe add a lovely twist to a classic gin and tonic, and are lifted by the spice notes of the star anise in this variation on the classic gin and tonic from Sipsmith.

Serves 1

ice cubes

25ml (1fl oz) Sipsmith London dry **gin**

25ml (1fl oz) Sipsmith **sloe gin**

25ml (1fl oz) good quality classic **tonic water**, or **lemon tonic water**

1 **star anise**

Fill a highball glass with ice. Add the gins (they will cool as they drizzle down the ice), top up with the tonic. Serve garnished with a star anise.

Star anise (*Illicium verum*) from Chaumeton: *Flore Médicale*, 1832.

BERRY SPICE

Something to take you off to the Caribbean, this luscious mixture from Peyton & Byrne of spiced rum and tangy fruit is great for a hot summer's evening.

Serves 1

ice cubes

35ml (1½fl oz) **spiced rum**

100ml (3½fl oz) fresh **cranberry juice**

50ml (2fl oz) **ginger ale**

a dash of **lime juice**

a wedge of **lime**, to serve

Place the ice in a tall glass. Add all the ingredients, except the wedge of lime. Stir, and then add the wedge of lime. Serve immediately.

Cranberry (*Vaccinium oxycoccos*) from Oeder et al: *Flora Danica*, 1761-1883.

LIMONCELLO FIZZ

The lemon grass and lemon zest can be removed after muddling and before adding the ice and tonic water, to produce a soft, citrus flavour. However, leaving them in the glass intensifies the flavour, which is fantastically refreshing, especially on a very hot, summer day. Any kind of lemons can be used, but the Italian varieties, such as Amalfi, are much more flavoursome and are usually un-waxed. Keep a bottle of limoncello handy in the freezer and add a splash to liven up a lemon drizzle cake, fruit fools or stewed fruits, such as apple or rhubarb.

1. Place the lemon grass and lemon zest in a tall glass and muddle lightly with a muddler or wooden spoon.
2. Fill the glass three quarters full with ice and pour over the Limoncello. Top up with tonic water. Add a straw, and serve.

Serves 1

2.5-cm (1-in) piece
lemon grass
a pared strip of Amalfi
lemon zest
ice cubes
1 x 25ml (1fl oz) shot
limoncello
200ml (7fl oz) **tonic water**

Lemon (*Citrus* x *limon*)
from Poiteau: *Pomologie Française*, 1846.

OPIUM POPPY OLD FASHIONED

Throughout history, the poppy has been used as a narcotic for its euphoric and painkilling attributes. Its sap produces opium from which morphine, codeine and heroin are extracted. Cultivated as far back as 3,400BC in the Middle East, Afghanistan still produces the world's largest quantity of opium. Eating a couple of spoonfuls of poppy seeds will definitely constitute a positive result on a drug test. You've been warned.

Serves 1

30ml (1fl oz) **bourbon**

15ml (½fl oz) **poppy seed infusion***

40ml (1½fl oz) **grapefruit juice**

20ml (¾fl oz) **tamarind Sugar Syrup****

1 tsp **lemon juice**

1 dash **angostura bitters**

ice cubes

To serve:

a slice of **lemon**

poppy seeds

1. Place all the ingredients in a cocktail shaker with a handful of ice, and shake hard for ten seconds.
2. Rub a slice of lemon around the outer rim of an old-fashioned glass and then roll the wet part of the glass in a saucer of poppy seeds. Add some fresh ice to the glass and strain the cocktail over it. Serve immediately.

* To make the poppy seed infusion: combine 500ml (17fl oz) Bulleit bourbon whiskey with 100g (4oz) toasted white poppy seeds and allow to infuse for a few days.

** To make the tamarind sugar syrup: pour 2.5 litres (4½ pints) of water into a large saucepan and add 1.5kg (3lb) granulated sugar. Heat the water gently, stirring constantly until the sugar has dissolved. Allow to cool and add 120g (4oz) tamarind paste. Store the syrup in a lidded container in the fridge and use as desired.

Lemon
Citrus x limon

Poppy (*Papaver bracteatum*) by unknown Indian artist, Company School, probably late 18th century.

Papaver
bracteatum

THREE FRUIT MARY

Inspired by Scott Beattie's take on a Bloody Mary, this sophisticated version combines three varieties of tomato and the spices of No. 3 London dry gin. The different cherry tomatoes each contribute their own flavours and colours to this visually stunning drink. Sip while contemplating the day of gardening ahead.

Serves 1

15 small **green basil leaves**

15 small **purple basil leaves**

50ml (2 fl oz) **No. 3 London dry gin**

50ml (2fl oz) **Isle of Wight tomato water***

3 **Piccolo cherry tomatoes, halved**

3 **Solana golden cherry tomatoes, halved**

3 **lemonade cherry tomatoes, halved**

15ml (½fl oz) **lemon juice**

¾tsp **oak roasted tomato infused balsamic vinegar**

¼tsp **sea salt**

⅓tsp **black pepper**

To serve:

½ **lemon** for rim

red sea salt, to serve

ice cubes

1. Prepare a high ball glass by rubbing the lemon half around the rim and dipping the rim into the red salt to coat it.

2. 'Spank', or slightly bruise, both types of basil and then drop them into a mixing glass or jug. Add the gin, tomato water, tomatoes, lemon juice, vinegar and salt and pepper, and stir well.

3. Add enough ice to fill the mixing glass or jug, stir until chilled and then pour the cocktail into the prepared high ball glass.

4. Garnish by stirring some of the halved tomatoes and red and green basil leaves through the glass.

* To make the isle of Wight tomato water: blend 225g (about ½lb) Isle of Wight tomatoes with 25g (1oz) salt until smooth, then strain through several layers of muslin cloth. It will take about 12 hours to drain fully and should be completely clear.

Tomatoes (*Solanum lycopersicum*) from *Album Benary*, 1876–82.

Black pepper
Piper nigrum

THE WALLED GARDEN

For anyone lucky enough to have roses in their garden, this simple cocktail is ideal to drink while sitting and enjoying the late afternoon or early evening sunshine and the smell of the roses. It was inspired by the rose collection at Wakehurst, which can be found in the walled garden.

Pour the ingredients into a chilled martini glass and stir well. Garnish with one or two rose water crackers, and serve.

Serves 1
50ml (2 fl oz) **Grey Goose vodka** or any other premium vodka, chilled
25ml (1 fl oz) **rose water**
rose water crackers, to serve

Engravings from Johann Christoph Volkamer's *Nürnbergische Hesperides*, 1708–14, feature charming perspective drawings of gardens and views showing the places where he collected many citrus and pomegranate fruits.

Des Herren von Lempen Hauß-Garten.

MINT JULEP

The mint julep is traditionally associated with the southern states of the USA.
In particular, it is served at the Kentucky Derby. But you don't need to travel that
far to enjoy it.

Serves 1

3–4 sprigs of **mint**

1 tbsp **caster sugar**

2½ tbsp water

180ml (6fl oz) **bourbon** or any
    rye whiskey or **cognac**

crushed ice

orange slices or **fruit berries**
    of your choice (optional, to
    serve)

a dash of **Jamaica rum**

caster sugar, to serve

1. Place the mint, water and sugar in a large glass, and press
   the mint well.

2. Add the bourbon or other rye whisky or cognac and some
   crushed ice.

3. Take out the mint and turn it upside down and reinsert it in
   the glass like a bouquet. Add the orange slices and berries
   (if using) and a dash of Jamaica rum. Sprinkle some sugar
   on the top, and serve.

Orange
Citrus aurantium

Sugar cane (*Saccharum officinarum*) from Köhler: *Medizinal Pflanzen*,
1883–1914.

20 BELOW

One of the projects that has been worked on by Kew's Millennium Seed Bank team at Wakehurst is the UK National Tree Seed Project (UKNTSP) in partnership with Forest Research, the UK Forestry Commission's research agency. To do its bit for our future gin and tonics juniper seed is being collected from across the UK. This is stored at minus 20°C. Enjoy this homage to the juniper.

Serves 1

40ml (1½oz) **white rum** or **gin**

25ml (1fl oz) **juniper simple syrup**

15ml (½fl oz) **lemon juice**

25ml (1fl oz) **pineapple juice**

To serve:

ice cubes

juniper berries and **rosemary sprigs** (optional, to garnish – if gin is used)

1. Place all the ingredients in a cocktail shaker. Put the lid on and shake to mix well.

2. Put some ice cubes in a wine glass and pour over the cocktail. Garnish with a few juniper berries and the rosemary sprig, if using. Serve.

* To make the juniper simple syrup, crush 25g (1oz) of juniper berries in a pestle and mortar. Then add the crushed berries to a saucepan with 600ml (1 pt) of water and 120g (4oz) of sugar and gentle boil for three hours. The liquid will reduce to a runny syrup. Allow the syrup to cool, and leave it in the fridge overnight. Double strain the syrup and then use as required.

Juniper (*Juniperus communis*) from Köhler: *Medizinal Pflanzen*, 1883-1914.

The UKNTSP is collecting seeds from 50 woody species that have been selected for their conservation importance and prevalence in the landscape. The common juniper, native to Britain, is one of these target species and is particularly vulnerable to *Phytophthora austrocedrae*, which causes severe dieback. In 2013, seeds from 24 juniper populations were collected from Scotland and parts of northern and southern England and in 2014 approximately 37 more juniper collections were added, including some from Wales. The juniper seeds are stored in the Millennium Seed Bank at -20°C.

PARADISE MARTINI

The inspiration for this drink from The Gin Garden is the fantastically named spice grains of paradise (*Aframomum melegueta*). The spice, part of the ginger family, Zingiberaceae, is also known as Melegueta alligator pepper or Guinea grains and is obtained from the ground seeds. It has a pungent, peppery flavour with hints of citrus. The 47 gin botanicals, tea and bergamot create an exotic twist on the well-known Earl Grey Martini.

Serves 1

50ml (2fl oz) **Monkey 47 gin**

35ml (1¼fl oz) best quality **Earl Grey tea** (containing real **bergamot**)

15ml (½ fl oz) fresh **pomelo juice**

15ml (½ fl oz) Home-made **bergamot and grains of paradise syrup***

½ **egg white**

To serve:

pomelo foam**

edible flowers such as jasmine or geranium petals, or a slice of pomelo or grapefruit peel

1. Place a martini glass in the freezer to chill.
2. Combine the gin, tea, pomelo juice and syrup in a cocktail shaker and shake well.
3. Strain the cocktail twice into the chilled martini glass, and add a thin layer of pomelo foam on top. Garnish with a few jasmine or geranium petals or a twist of pomelo or grapefruit peel. Serve immediately.

* To make the bergamot and grains and paradise syrup, combine 125ml (4fl oz) water and 100g (4oz) caster sugar in a saucepan, heat and stir until clear. Add a teaspoon of grains of paradise and the peel of a bergamot (*Citrus bergamia*) to the saucepan and heat the syrup for a further 5–15 minutes. Leave the syrup to cool, then strain it through a muslin cloth. Store the syrup in the fridge.

** To make the pomelo foam: combine 1 x 12g sachet of powdered gelatine with 75ml (3fl oz) pomelo juice, 75ml (3fl oz) sugar syrup (see page 50) and 75ml (3fl oz) coconut milk. Mix thoroughly and dispense from a whipped cream canister. Visit www.gingarden.com for more detailed instructions.

CHILLIES

by Sheila Keating

What is mildly addictive, has a rock band named after it, has been used in hangover cures, as a currency and even to ward off elephants? Answer: the chilli pepper.

The original home of the chilli has been much debated, with many pinpointing the Peruvian and Bolivian Andes. However, it is now thought that the earliest chillies were found growing wild in Mexico, where fragments of peppers dating back between 9,000 and 7,000 years were discovered in the Tehuacán Valley in the state of Puebla, in central eastern Mexico, and in the Ocampo caves in Tamaulipas in the north east of the country. The three great South American civilisations – the Mayans, Aztecs and Incas – revered the chilli – and the name itself comes from the Aztec Nahuatl language. The Aztecs were also early pioneers of the power of chilli and chocolate (which they considered the food of the gods) in a bitter, dark and spicy drink.

Chillies belong to the *Capsicum* genus, which is part of the larger nightshade family Solanaceae that also includes potatoes, tomatoes and aubergines. Most modern cultivars belong to just three species. The main one is *Capsicum annuum*, which includes most of the best-known varieties, such as the jalepeño, poblano and serrano and the bell pepper, which has no heat. The other two major species are *Capsicum frutescens*, which includes the 'Tabasco', Thai bird's eye and Portuguese piri piri chillies, and *Capsicum chinense* that encompasses the fiery habanero and Scotch Bonnet. All in all, there are several thousand varieties of chillies, many of which are local to certain regions because they cross-pollinate easily, and what a colourful, diverse and captivating collection they make, ranging from the small and bulbous to the long and pointed or prettily lantern-shaped. They might be glossily smooth or dimpled and wrinkled, with colours that span through yellow to lime green and emerald,

or crimson to purpley-brown. Of course, each has its own distinctive fruity flavour in addition to heat. And then there are the splendid names: 'Hungarian Hot Wax', 'Trinidad Scorpion', 'Naga Viper', Infinity...

Every spice-loving community worldwide has its traditional and favourite varieties. In general, India tends to use either long fresh green chillies —whole, or slit lengthways — or smaller dried red ones, which might be ground. Piri piri is the classic Portuguese and South African pepper, while in Thai cooking the smaller the chilli, the hotter: witness the bird's eye, the most lethal of which is the *phrik khi nu suan*.

It was Christopher Columbus who brought chillies to Europe in the 15th century — most likely the 'bird' or tabasco variety—which were named 'peppers', as the heat they produced was considered similar to that of peppercorns. Technically, they are actually the berries of the chilli plant — a hollow fruit whose seeds are enclosed in the pericarp (wall) of a single ovary. So contrary to our common culinary perception, a chilli is a berry, while a strawberry or raspberry, strictly, is not.

In Europe, the newly discovered peppers were first grown by monks in Portugal in Spain, from where they spread via trading networks to India and Southeast Asia, and on to the Middle East and the rest of Europe. Despite the famous British love of curry, with its roots in colonial days, it is only in the last few decades that fresh and dried chillies in every colour, shape and variety have begun brightening up everything from ice creams to cocktails.

So where does the heat come from? Over 40 different compounds have been identified in chillies, but their fieriness is determined by chemicals known as capsaicinoids, the main ones being capsaicin and dihydrocapsaicin, which are concentrated in the membrane surrounding the seeds. Their levels can vary according to the region where the chillies are grown, the soil, climate and maturity of the fruit. Capsaicinoids trigger a rush of endorphins (the body's natural painkillers) which can produce a feeling of mild euphoria, so it is no wonder that most chilli lovers talk about being addicted to

the sensation. In New Mexico, where chillies are on the menu from breakfast to dinner, it is said they are the secret not only of happiness, but also of long life, perhaps because they are a great source of vitamin C and vitamin A.

There is however, a fine line between the pleasure of a spicily fruity chilli and the pain of one that sets your mouth ablaze. A chilli's heat is measured in Scoville Heat Units (SHUs) named after an American pharmacist, Wilbur Scoville, who developed a test in 1912 which involved diluting the extract of the chilli in sugar syrup until it became undetectable. However many scientists felt this to be flawed, as it relied on the human perception of heat, so the more recent and objective method is to use high performance liquid chromatography to determine the concentration of heat-producing chemicals in the fruit.

Nevertheless, much machismo is expended on growing and attempting to eat chillies that register record-breaking fieriness on the SHU scale. First the Red Savina, which reached 577,000 units, was considered the hottest chilli in the world, then the record tumbled to the 'Bhut Jolokia', which shattered a million units, followed by the 'Naga Viper' and the 'Trinidad Scorpion'. Since 2013 the Carolina Reaper, a variety of *Capsicum chinense*, has held the title, registering a terrifying 2,200,000 on the scale (by way of comparison, a jalapeño pepper records a mere 3,500-10,000 units).

Back in 1597, the herbalist Nicholas Culpeper warned, in his *Complete Herbal* that chillies would:

> 'burn and inflame the mouth and throat so extremely that it is hard to be endured, and if it be outwardly applied to the skin in any part of the body, it will exulcerate and raise it as if it had been burnt with fire, or scalded with hot water'.

He did, however, acknowledge that while these were the dangers of the 'immoderate use of these violent plants and fruits', when 'corrected of their evil qualities, they are of considerable service', though as a remedy for various ailments, rather than for eating — something the peoples of the Americas had discovered long ago. It is said that the Mayans used peppers

to treat sore throats and coughs, while the Native American Indians used them to treat everything from toothache and fever to scorpion stings. The Mayans and Aztecs are also reported to have burned chillies in order to use their smoke to sting the eyes of enemies (like today's defensive pepper sprays which also contain capsaicin). And in some parts of Africa and India, farmers planted chillies around their crops or burned a mixture of chillies and cow dung to keep away elephants, whose highly developed sense of smell makes them particularly sensitive to capsaicin.

True chilli lovers, however, take the lead from their home, Mexico, where complexity of flavour is valued over sheer heat. Although the mainstay is the jalapeño, many recipes will call for the milder poblano, as well as the hotter habanero. Or they will blend different varieties, sometimes using a combination of fresh and dried chillies, which often have a richer more raisin-like character, or chipotles (smoked jalapeños).

Chillies may hail from warm, dry regions, but are one of only a few spice crops that can be cultivated in very different climates around the world — from temperate to tropical. In the last two decades, British gardeners have woken up to the joys of growing chillies in kitchen gardens and on patios in addition to greenhouses. At Kew, as well as being grown in its glass houses, they flourish outdoors in the *Kew on a Plate* Kitchen Garden where they provide vibrant splashes of colour through summer and into autumn. Particularly spectacular is the ornamental, medium-hot 'NuMex Twilight', originally from Jalisco, Mexico and one of many popular cultivars that have been developed at the New Mexico State University as part of their on-going chilli research programme. It produces masses of tiny, upwardly-pointing peppers, maturing from purple through to yellow, orange and finally red at different stages, a wonderful multi-coloured display.

Chillies (*Capsicum annuum*) from *Album Benary*, 1876–82.

THE WORLD'S HOTTEST BLOODY MARIA

This tequila-based version of the Bloody Mary is a mouthful of smokey notes and a real hit of fiery heat, courtesy of the world's hottest chilli pepper, the Carolina Reaper, a cross-breed of the Ghost Chilli and Red Habanero peppers. Ultimately, it's up to you how much to add, but be cautious. In this recipe, the chilli is balanced by the sweetness of the fragrant gherkin vinegar and the freshness of the fresh lime juice.

Serves 1

50ml (2fl oz) blanco **tequila**

200ml (7fl oz) fresh **tomato juice**

10ml (2 tsp) fresh **lime juice**

10ml (2 tsp) **gherkin vinegar**

a pinch of **smoked salt**

a generous knife point of **Carolina Reaper purée***

ice cubes

a few julienne slices of **chilli**, to serve

1. Combine all the ingredients except the chilli slices in a cocktail shaker with a handful of ice, and shake hard for ten seconds.
2. Strain the cocktail over fresh ice cubes in a high ball glass.
3. Garnish the drink by placing a few julienned slices of fresh chilli on the surface of the drink (skin the chillies, slice them thinly and place them in iced water and they will curl up nicely).

* To make the purée: chop up 1 Carolina Reaper chilli and blend it in a food processor. Just dip the tip of a knife into the purée and bring out a little amount to add to the cocktail.

Chilli (*Capsicum annuum*) from Köhler: *Medizinal Pflanzen*, 1883–1914.

COUPETTE NO. 3

Chillies and other spices are naturals in cocktails served either before or with Asian food, and this is a lovely refreshing drink created in the bar of the Japanese restaurant Sake no Hana in London's Mayfair. 'Working with spices in drinks is very satisfying. People really enjoy the gentle heat, which works with the heat of the alcohol to produce something quite complex' says Senior Bar Manager Eder Neto. 'How much chilli you add is really up to you, and depends on the strength of the flakes, so I suggest you add just a little to the vanilla sugar at first, then taste it and add more if you like.'

1. Chill a coupette glass in the freezer for half an hour before making the cocktail. Or, if you don't have time, while you are mixing the cocktail, fill the glass with ice and add soda water which will speed up the chilling process.
2. Put all of the ingredients into a cocktail shaker, and shake well.
3. Empty the chilled glass if you have used ice and soda water to cool it. Pour the cocktail through a fine strainer into the chilled glass. Serve immediately.

* For the ginger juice, grate a good wedge of fresh, peeled ginger root (about 3.5cm/1½in) and either it push through a fine sieve or squeeze through muslin.

** To make the vanilla and chilli sugar: blend 250g (8oz) caster sugar together with half a vanilla pod and a pinch of chilli flakes (to taste) in a food processor until you have a fine powder. Keep the sugar in an airtight jar and use as required.

Makes one cocktail

40 ml (1½ fl oz) traditionally distilled **gin**

50 ml (2fl oz) **grapefruit juice**

1 dessert spoon **ginger juice***

1 tsp **sugar syrup** (see page opposite)

1 tbsp **vanilla and chilli sugar****

ice cubes

Chilli (*Capsicum annuum*) from Régnault:
La Botanique Mise à la Portée de Tout le Monde, 1774.

CHILLI MARTINI

A favourite, luxurious cocktail from the Michelin-starred dim sum teahouse, Yauatcha, in London, this drink will really make you tingle.

1. Put all the ingredients except the champagne or sparkling wine into a cocktail shaker, and shake well.

2. Strain the cocktail through a fine sieve into the glass. Top up with the champagne or sparkling wine, and serve.

* To make the chilli sugar syrup: pour 60ml (2¼ fl oz) water into a small saucepan, and bring to the boil. Add 120g (4oz) caster sugar, and stir constantly until the sugar dissolves, forming a clear, light syrup. Allow the syrup to cool. Then blend the syrup with 1 long, hot, red chilli and pass the syrup through a fine sieve to remove the chilli seeds. It can be kept in a container in the fridge for up to 28 days.

Serves 1

25ml (1 fl oz) **vodka**

15ml (½ fl oz) **Campari**

25ml (1 fl oz) fresh **orange juice**

2 tsp **chilli sugar syrup***

ice cubes

35ml (1½ fl oz) **champagne** or other **méthode champenoise sparkling wine**

Orange
Citrus x *aurantium*

Chilli (*Capsicum annuum*) from Köhler: *Medizinal Pflanzen*, 1883–1914.

Ampelideae.

Grape Vine (*Vitis vinifera*) from Köhler: *Medizinal Pflanzen*, 1883–1914.

PARTY PUNCHES

Pineapple
Ananas comosus)
engraving from
Bertuch: *Bilderbuch
für Kinder*, 1798.

LONDON PUNCH

The word 'punch' comes from the Sanskrit word *'pancha'* meaning five. It is appropriate, as punch traditionally contained five ingredients: strong, weak, sweet, citrus and spice. Sailors travelling on the spice ships back to London picked up the taste for it, and by the 1800s, punches had become ubiquitous across London society. They were usually gin based and every public house would have had its own version, served out of a communal bowl and often grated with nutmeg on top.

Serves 10
ice cubes
500ml (17fl oz) Sipsmith
   London dry **gin** infused
   with **Assam tea**
250ml (8fl oz) **lemon juice**,
   freshly squeezed
250ml (8fl oz) **simple syrup**
pieces of **lemon peel**, to serve

1. To infuse the gin; add four heaped teaspoons of Assam tea leaves to a 70cl bottle of London dry gin. Leave the mixture for 45 minutes and then strain.

2. To make simple syrup; combine equal measures of sugar and water in an empty bottle. Shake occasionally. Within 15 minutes the sugar will dissolve.

3. Combine the ingredients in the specified quantities in a jug. Serve with ice and garnish with lemon peel.

Nutmeg (*Myristica fragrans*) from Stephenson and Churchill: *Medical Botany*, 1834-36.

PINEAPPLE PUNCH

A fabulous punch for a party, this recipe is adapted from Jerry Thomas's *Bartender's Guide*, which was originally published in 1862. The pineapple and rum flavours will certainly transport you to the Caribbean.

1. Place the pineapple and the caster sugar in a large glass bowl and let it stand until the sugar is soaked up by the pineapple juices.
2. Add all the other ingredients except the champagne and stand the bowl in ice for 1 hour. Then add the champagne.
3. Put a large block of ice in a fresh bowl, and pour the punch over this. Taste and add some extra sugar as desired. Then add the sliced seasonal fruits, and serve.

Serves 10

4 **pineapples**, peeled, cored and sliced
450g (1lb) **caster sugar** + extra, to taste
4 bottles of **champagne**
600ml (1pt) **Jamaica rum**
600ml (1pt) **brandy**
150ml (¼pt) **curaçao**
juice of 4 **lemons**
ice, including 1 large block
seasonal fruits, such as oranges, lemons, sliced

Pineapple (*Ananas comosus)* 'Lady Beatrice Lambton', by P. de Pannemaeker, after a drawing by C. T. Rosenberg, c.1850.

TRADITIONAL SPICED PUNCH

It's worth making the spiced syrup to give this punch from Sipsmith the extra dimension. You can keep any left over syrup in a bottle in the fridge.

Serves 10

ice cubes

250ml (8fl oz) simple **spiced syrup**

500ml (17fl oz) **Sipsmith London dry gin**

250ml (8fl oz) fresh squeezed **lemon juice**

250ml (8fl oz) **Sipsmith sloe gin**

To serve:

pieces of **lemon peel**

grated nutmeg

1. To make the spiced syrup, combine 1 litre (1 ¾pt) water with 1kg (2lb) caster sugar and a handful of spices of your choosing, such as star anise, cloves or cinnamon, in a saucepan. Place over a high heat and bring to the boil, then reduce the heat and simmer for a minimum of 15 minutes. After 15 minutes, the sugar should have dissolved. Leave to cool.

2. Place a ice cubes in a glass jug. Add all the ingredients, in the stated quantities and stir.

3. To serve pour into wine glasses (include the ice) and garnish with the lemon peel and a tiny amount of grated nutmeg.

Nutmeg
Myristica fragrans

Lemon (*Citrus* spp.) from Duhamel du Monceau: *Traité des arbres et arbustes*, Nouvelle édition, 1819.

CITRUS Bigaradia bizarro.   CITRONIER Bigaradier bizarre.

WINTER-SPICED NEGRONI

A negroni is not just for summer. This will cheer anyone up at any time of the year. Adjust the quantities below if you want to make less or more (the ratio is 1:1:1:3).

1. Put the Campari, sweet vermouth, gin, cider, orange juice and freshly ground spice in a saucepan and heat gently. Don't let it simmer.

2. When it's warm, carefully pour it into glasses and garnish with the slice of blood orange. Serve immediately.

* To make your own five-spice: toast 2 tsp star anise, 2 tsp fennel seeds, a cinnamon stick, 2 tsp Szechuan pepper and 2 tsp cloves. Grind the toasted spices together in a pestle and mortar or use a clean coffee grinder for a less laborious method. Make sure that they are thoroughly mixed together.

Serves 10

300ml (½pt) **Campari**

300ml (½pt) **sweet vermouth**

300ml (½pt) **gin**

900ml (1½pt) **cloudy cider** (not the fizzy sort – use a quality brand)

juice of 5 **blood oranges**

5tsp freshly ground **five-spice mix***

10 slices of **blood orange**, to garnish

Clove
Syzygium aromaticum

Orange (*Citrus* x *aurantium*) from Mordant De Launay and Loiseleur-Deslongchamps: *Herbier Général de l'Amateur*, vol. 7, 1817-1827.

NORMAN COURT GROG

Originally grog was made from rum diluted with boiled seawater and a squeeze of lemon or lime to hide the salty flavour. This grog recipe was used aboard the tea clipper *Norman Court* (wrecked off Wales in 1883) and was given to Jonathan Farley, Conservator at Kew, by a descendant of one of the sailors, who also acted as ship's cook. It differs substantially from the 'Naval Grog' of the same period, which had only gone so far as to substitute boiled sea water with fresh water.

Serves 6

3 tsp **granulated sugar**
300ml (½pt) boiling **water**
150ml (¼pt) fresh **orange juice**
85ml (3fl oz) fresh **lemon juice**
180ml (6fl oz) fresh **lime juice**
180ml (6fl oz) **dark rum**

The tea clipper *Norman Court*

1. Place the sugar in a heatproof jug, add the boiling water and allow it to dissolve. Leave the jug in the fridge to cool overnight.
2. Add the fruit juices and the rum. Store in the fridge, and consume within a few days. In the summer, you can serve it chilled over ice with a sprig of mint, or in winter, try it with the cinnamon variation (see below) served warm in the style of mulled wine.

Try a couple of variations:

- Substitute the juice of two pomegranates for the six limes. It is rather fiddly to juice a pomegranate, however, so you can use grenadine from a bottle instead, but dilute (120ml (4 fl oz) with 50ml (2 fl oz)of water, otherwise it will be too strong.
- Add a pinch of cinnamon to the water before bringing it to the boil and mixing it with the sugar.

GROG was first introduced into the Royal Navy by Vice-Admiral Edward Vernon in 1740. Vernon wore a coat of grogram cloth and was nicknamed *Old Grogram* or *Old Grog*, from which the drink's name derives. Grog served three purposes: first, it provided an energy boost to the weary sailors, who in the most blustery seas could easily go for days without sleep. Second, the alcohol acted as a mild anaesthetic to ease weary limbs, but was not sufficient to make a sailor incapable, and finally, the citrus content of the drink prevented scurvy. One of America's nicknames for the British is 'Limey' because of Britain's use of limes on board ship. Similarly, Australians use the term 'Pom' because pomegranates were generally substituted for limes on the wool clippers, which were easier to acquire on that route.

RUM BUTTER PUNCH FOR TWELFTH NIGHT

This recipe from Gina Fullerlove is an ideal winter's eve treat, not just for the last night of Christmas, to share with loved ones.

1. Place all the ingredients, except the nutmeg, in a saucepan, and heat to just below boiling point, stirring with spoon until the butter has melted and emulsified in the liquid.

2. Check for taste, adding more butter and syrup or honey to taste.
   Serve hot.

Serves 10

25g (1oz) **unsalted butter**

1-2 tbsp **maple syrup** or **honey**

2-3 tsp ground **allspice**

250ml (8fl oz) **rum**

1.5 litres (2½pt) **apple juice**

2 **cinnamon sticks**

freshly grated **nutmeg**, to garnish (optional)

Cinnamon (*Cinnamomum zeylanicum*) from Köhler: *Medizinal Pflanzen*, 1883–1914.

MULLED WINE

The pungent smell of mulled wine being prepared never fails to lift the spirits and cannot be bettered when coming in from the outside on a cold and damp winter's day. Here is Gina Fullerlove's recipe.

Serves 5

750ml (1¼pt) bottle of
   red wine

300ml (½pt) **water**

6cm (2½in) **cinnamon stick**

4 **cloves**

4 **green cardamom pods**,
   gently crushed to release
   the seeds

2 **star anise**

1 tsp **juniper berries**

finely pared rind of ¼ **lemon**

about 75g (3oz) **sugar**, to taste

1. Place all the ingredients except the sugar in a covered saucepan and heat gently to a simmer, add the sugar and continue to cook on a very low heat for 10-15 minutes, to let the spices to infuse. Do not allow the wine to boil.

2. Taste for sweetness and add more sugar if needed, then strain into a jug. It is wonderful served with roasted, salted, hot chestnuts, homemade cheese straws or Christmas fruit cake.

Juniper
Juniperus communis

Vine *(Vitis vinifera)* from Poiteau:
Pomologie Française, 1846.

RUMFUSTIAN

In his 1862 *Bartender's Guide*, Jerry Thomas describes this drink as being 'in vogue with English sportsmen, after their return from a day's shooting'. You don't need to have gone shooting, but this Rumfustian will certainly warm anyone up after a long walk on a cold, crisp day.

1. In a large jug or bowl, whisk the egg yolks together with the beer and gin.
2. Pour the bottle of sherry into a large saucepan and add the cinnamon, nutmeg, sugar lumps and the lemon rind. Bring the mixture to the boil.
3. Pour the hot mixture into the mixture of eggs, gin and beer and stir. Serve hot.

Makes approximately
2.4 litres (4 pints)

12 **egg yolks**
1 litre (1¾pt) **strong beer**
600ml (1pt) **gin**
750ml (1¼pt) bottle of **medium sherry**
1 **cinnamon stick**
1 **nutmeg**, grated
12 lumps of **sugar**

LAURUS CASSIA L.
Die Cassie.

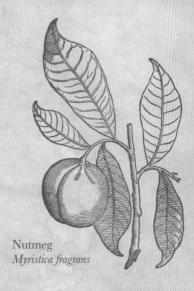

Nutmeg
Myristica fragrans

Cinnamon (*Cinnamomum verum*)
from Plenck: *Icones Plantarum
Medicinalium*, 1788–1812.

BITTERS

by Jason Irving

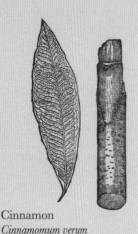

Bitter is often described as the 'forgotten flavour' because although it is fundamental to the range of human taste, it is often avoided. However, it may be making a comeback, as bitters are making a welcome return to cocktail menus.

According to its most basic definition, a cocktail is simply a mix of two or more drinks, one of which contains alcohol. This simple premise proves to be an endless source of intoxicating concoctions — blending spirits, liqueurs, cordials and juices made from a whole array of herbs, spices and fruits. In search of the best way to get their customers deliciously drunk, mixologists are returning to the classics for inspiration, spurring the recent renaissance in the cocktail as old favourites take on new twists. Looking beyond the simple and the sweet for the complex and unusual, and inspired by the chemistry of cooking, these new cocktails are exploring the full range of the human palate. This has led to the rediscovery of the importance of cocktail bitters — plant extracts that add an extra depth of flavour and balance sweetness.

These extracts were fundamental to the original cocktail as shown in the first written definition that appeared in an American weekly magazine in 1808: 'Cock-tail is a stimulating liquor, composed of spirits of any kind, sugar, water, and bitters'. This is why the basic blend of whisky, sugar and bitters is known as an 'Old Fashioned', but the history of bitters goes back further.

Bitters began life as medicinal preparations made from many different plants that became the classic cure-all tonics, widely available in pharmacies in the 18th and 19th centuries. At some point, they began to be mixed with spirits and drunk for pleasure, probably as a way to dilute the strong flavour of the medicine that developed into an excuse for getting drunk. This is the possible origin of the classic British cocktail; soldiers stationed in India

Angelica
Angelica archangelica

Cinnamon
Cinnamomum verum

Burdock
Arctium lappa

had to drink regular doses of cinchona bark to protect them against malaria, and to mask its unpleasant flavour, they mixed it with gin and lemon, thus creating the gin and tonic.

Unearthing the roots of bitter tonics throws up many such stories, revealing a fascinating history of the medicinal use of plants. By returning to herbal medicine and discovering the traditional uses of local plants, we can find clues as to where to look for new flavouring ideas and gain an understanding of the elements that make up bitters.

Herbal medicines are often unpleasantly bitter because they are concentrated extracts of parts of plants that we would not normally eat in large amounts. However, bitterness also serves a therapeutic function that has been recognised for thousands of years. Bitter taste receptors on the tongue send signals to the digestive tract that cause the release of a range of digestive juices and increase the movement of the gut wall. While the complexities of this mechanism are still being untangled, basically a dose of bitters acts as a wake-up call, kicking the whole digestive system into gear.

As a result, bitter leaves, barks and roots are employed in many different herbal traditions to treat digestive complaints ranging from infections to poor appetite and general indigestion. Wormwood (*Artemisia absinthium*) gets its name from its ability to kill intestinal parasites, and its medicinal use led to the development of vermouth (the German name for the plant is 'vermut') and absinthe.

The effect of bitter taste on the appetite is the origin of the *aperitivo* hour in Italy, when drinks such as Campari, Aperol, and vermouth are drunk before a meal. This idea of an *aperitivo* has even been traced back to Greece in 400 AD. Many traditional medicinal bitter preparations survive as aromatised spirits in Europe, such as *Kräuterlikör* ('herb liquor') in Germany, *Alpenbitter* in Switzerland, or *amaro* in Italy. These are drunk on their own, but there is a great range of different variations available in different localities. The British seem to be content with their gin and tonic, or perhaps it is because they prefer to take their bitters in the form of beer.

Walnut
Jugla regia

Fennel
Foeniculum vulgare

Orange
Citrus x *aurantium*

Almond
Prunus dulcis

Lemon
Citrus x *limon*

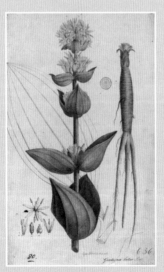

Yellow gentian (*Gentiana lutea*)
from the Kew Collection.

The preparations known as 'cocktail bitters' are closely linked to the Americas, where in the hands of enterprising advertisers 'bitters' became the name for a whole range of health boosting tonics. The most commonly known is Angostura bitters, developed by a German doctor in Venezuela in 1824 to help the soldiers of Simón Bolívar's army deal with stomach ache. It was eventually added to cocktails and thereafter bitters were developed specifically for this use; recent years have seen a proliferation of bitters producers.

All these bitter preparations have their historical roots in local monasteries, then pharmacies that would use a variety of local herbs to make their medicines. The plants were dried and steeped in alcohol to extract and preserve their medicinal properties.

The bitterness can come from roots, leaves or barks. One of the most commonly used bittering agents is the root of yellow gentian (*Gentiana lutea*) that grows in the mountains of central and southern Europe. Although it contains one of the bitterest compounds known, amarogentin, the flavour of the root extract is more complex, with layers of different bitters, a sweetness and even a slight floral note. Many bitter roots also have sweet elements because the roots are where a plant stores sugars. Other plants with subterranean parts that lend themselves to bitters include chicory, often used as a coffee substitute, dandelion and burdock, originally taken together as a spring tonic, and angelica, an important component of gin and other spirits.

Barks contain chemicals called tannins which taste bitter but are also astringent. This effect of tightening the tissues of the mouth adds texture to a blend, and is why wine is aged in oak wood barrels. All the barks that have been used in bitters have a history of medicinal use, such as cinchona bark for treating malaria, willow bark for treating arthritis, and oak bark for treating sore throat.

A wide range of medicinal plants – often aromatic spices such as fennel, cinnamon, aniseed, angelica and cardamom – were added to the fundamental bitter elements. These spices have a high essential oil content that gives them their strong flavour and explains their use in herbal medicine as carminatives that settle the digestive tract by reducing the build-up of wind and producing an antimicrobial action. This is why they are the more dominant component in the mix of digestives — liqueurs drunk after a meal to settle the stomach. They were probably added to the blends of bitters because of their digestive use and to make the medicine more palatable. Although not as widely used medicinally, the rind of citrus fruit, particularly orange and grapefruit, have become popular in cocktail bitters, as they combine both the bitter and aromatic elements in one.

Many plants can be used to make bitters and each has an interesting tale to tell and a robust, intense flavour to add depth to many a cocktail. If you wish, you can make your own bitters.

Wormwood (*Artemisia absinthium*) from Plenck: *Icones Plantarum Medicinalium*, 1788–1812.

How to make bitters

Bitters are basically a type of tincture, commonly used in Western herbal medicine. A tincture is made by steeping dried, cut plants in alcohol, leaving them to infuse for anything from a day to several months, and then straining out the plant material and storing the liquid. The alcohol acts a solvent, extracting and concentrating the chemicals to make them easier to take, and as a preservative to ensure a ready, stable supply of medicine.

You can use any spirit, though plainer ones such as vodka will give you more control over the final flavour. There is a complex science to understanding which flavours extract best in different strengths based on the charge of the particular chemicals, but generally a stronger alcohol (40–60%) is preferable.

Selected the plants you wish to use, pack them into a large jar and cover them with alcohol. The optimum extraction time varies widely between different plants, so carry out a taste test after 12 hours, a day, two days and so on. Then strain the infused liquid into a bottle. Some bitters recipes mix many plants in one jar, but to create the optimum blend, make separate tinctures, and then experiment with different ratios until you discover the mix that works for you.

Cherries (*Prunus*) from Poiteau:
Pomologie Française, 1846.

Royale hâtive.

FIZZY CELEBRATION DRINKS

Orange (*Citrus x aurantium*) from
Risso and Poiteau: *Histoire et
Culture des Orangers*, 1782.

ORANGE PYRIFORME

Oranger Pyriforme

Tab. 7.

MARMALADE-ADE

Use regular oranges when blood oranges are out of season; they may be rather sweeter, so adjust the amount of juice and zest to taste. Homemade marmalade is by far the tastiest to use, with the strongest citrus flavour, so make the most of the Seville orange season in late January and early February and stock up for the year ahead.

Serves 6–8

3 tbsp chunky **Seville orange marmalade**

finely grated zest of 1 **blood orange**

juice of 2 **blood oranges**

1 x 75cl bottle **Asti Spumante**, well chilled

To serve:

thinly pared zest of 1 **blood orange**

2 **blood oranges**, segmented

1. Put the marmalade, grated orange zest and juice in a jug and muddle with a muddler, until soft and pulpy. Pour in the chilled Asti Spumante and stir to mix.

2. Strain the mixture through a fine sieve, into a chilled carafe.

3. Add the pared orange zest and blood orange segments to the carafe and serve.

Orange tree (*Citrus* x *aurantium*) from Risso and Poiteau: *Histoire et Culture des Orangers*, 1782.

ANGELS' BREATH

This pale pink confection of a drink is perfect for a summer celebration, such as a wedding or christening. Reminiscent of an archetypal English country garden, pelargonium leaves make for a very natural, herbal flavour, but if unavailable, rose petals alone will scent the cocktail beautifully, although it may make it taste rather sweeter. The size of pelargonium leaves will vary, so adjust the quantity used, according to personal taste and how perfumed a cocktail you prefer.

Pelargonium (*Pelargonium dioicum*) from *Curtis's Botanical Magazine*, 1821.

1. To prepare the rims of six champagne saucers: place the beaten egg white into a shallow dish large enough for the rims of the serving glasses to fit and be immersed slightly. Do the same with the caster sugar. Dip the rim of each champagne saucer first into the egg white and then into the caster sugar. This will give you a pretty frosted edge on each one.

2. Place the pelargonium leaves, white currants, sugar cube and rose liqueur in a cocktail shaker or jug and squash well with a muddler or a wooden spoon, until soft and pulpy. Strain the mixture through a fine sieve or tea strainer into the prepared glasses. Then fill each one with sparkling wine.

3. To serve: hang a small string of white currants over the side of each glass and float a rose petal on top of each. Serve immediately.

Serves 6

4 **scented pelargonium leaves***

a large handful **white currants**, stripped from the stems

4 tbsp **rose liqueur**

1 white **sugar cube**

1 x 750ml (1¼pt) bottle **brut rosé English sparkling wine**, well chilled

To serve:

Beaten **egg white**

caster sugar

6 small strings of **white currants**

6 pink scented **rose petals**

* we recommend 'Attar of Roses' a variety of scent-leaved pelargonium (*Pelargonium capitatum*)

RED CHERRY CARNIVAL

The deep red colour of fresh cherry purée paired with celebratory bubbles and served in tall frosty glasses feels both exotic and celebratory. Making this cocktail at the height of the cherry season, when the fruits are at their darkest and sweetest, will add an almost peppery hint to the mix. Place the flutes in the freezer for 10 minutes before serving the cocktail to create the pretty, frosted appearance.

Serves 6

100g (4oz) **dark red cherries**, pitted

40ml (1½ fl oz) **cherry brandy**

a couple of dashes of **bitters**

sugar syrup, to taste (see page 50)

1 x 75cl bottle **brut cava**, well chilled

To serve:

6 'pairs' of **red cherries**, on the stem

6 **mint sprigs**

1. Roughly chop the cherries and place them in a small bowl. Add the cherry brandy and bitters and process to a smooth purée, using a hand blender.

2. Taste the purée and add a little sugar syrup, if necessary. This will depend on personal taste and the natural sweetness of the cherries.

3. Divide the cherry purée between six tall flutes and top up with chilled cava.

4. Hang a 'pair' of cherries over the side of each glass and float a little sprig of mint on top of each serving.

5. Place the flutes in the freezer for ten minutes before serving the cocktail, to give them a pretty, frosted appearance.

Cherry (*Prunus*) from
Duhamel du Monceau:
Traité des Arbres et Arbustes, 1755.

STRAWBERRY, BASIL & ST GERMAIN CRUSH

Fragoli is a strawberry liqueur made from tiny, wild Alpine strawberries and St Germain is a wonderfully aromatic, alcoholic elderflower liqueur. In truth, neither is actually necessary for this cocktail, but they are both incredibly decadent and delicious! If unavailable, just use the fresh strawberries and add a splash of (ideally, homemade) elderflower cordial instead (see page 65).

1. Place the strawberries and basil leaves in a jug and muddle with a muddler or wooden spoon, until soft and pulpy.
2. Add the St Germain and Fragoli and muddle again, then, strain the mixture into a chilled carafe.
3. Pour the Prosecco into the carafe and stir gently to mix. Taste, and add a little sugar syrup, if desired.
4. Place a borage and elderflower ice cube into each of eight Martini glasses with a couple of Alpine strawberries (if using). Pour over the Strawberry and St Germain Crush and serve.

Serves 8

300g (10oz) small **strawberries**, hulled

2 large **basil leaves**

60ml (2½fl oz) **St Germain**

60ml (2½fl oz) **fragoli**

1 x 750ml (1¼pt) bottle **prosecco**, well chilled

1–2 tbsp **sugar syrup** (see page 50)

To serve:

borage and elderflower ice cubes*

alpine strawberries, optional

* To make these, mix elderflower cordial with water in a ratio of 1 to 4, pour into an ice cube container and drop one small borage flower (*Borago officinalis*) into each cube mould and freeze.

Strawberry (*Potentilla (Fragaria) ananassa*) from Besler: *Hortus Eystettensis*, 1613.

Fraga fructu albo.

MRS BEETON'S CLARET CUP

This simple recipe for a wine-based cup or punch from Mrs Beeton's archive makes a great base to experiment with variations and additional ingredients of your choice. Try adding some slices of seasonal fruit to add to the look of the punch if you are making it for a special occasion.

Serves approximately 12

a 750ml (1½pt) bottle of **claret**

1 bottle **soda water**

4 tbsp **icing sugar**

¼ tsp grated **nutmeg**

30ml (1fl oz) of **cherry brandy**

a sprig of green **borage**

225g (8oz) **crushed ice**

1. Put all the ingredients except the ice into a large bowl or punch bowl, and stir gently.
2. Add the ice. Don't add a lot if the general temperature is cold. If the weather is very warm, you can add more, as you wish.

Nutmeg
Myristica fragrans

Borage *(Borago officinalis)* from
Thomé: *Flora von Deutschland
Österreich und der Schweiz*, 1885.

RHUBARB ROSE

This drink uses the unusual rhubarb vodka as its base. Herefordshire rhubarb (*Rheum x hybridum*) is slowly cooked before being marinated with rhubarb vodka. The natural scent of rhubarb and custard is spiced with ginger and perfumed with rose to create a delicate, romantic drink.

1. Put the vodka, lemon juice and syrup in a mixing glass (or jug), add ice and stir.
2. Place the rhubarb chunks, rose petals and mint in a high ball glass. Then pour over the contents of the mixing glass and top up with sparkling water.
3. Garnish the drink by cutting a very fine strip of fresh rhubarb and curling it around a straw. Spritz the drink with the aromatic Rosa damascena aromatic rose water as desired.

* To make the home-made syrup: combine 125ml (4 fl oz) water and 100g (4oz) caster sugar in a saucepan, heat and stir until clear. Add 1 vanilla pod, the peel of 1 orange and a 4cm (1½in) piece of ginger, peeled and cut up, to the saucepan and and heat for a further 5–15 minutes. Leave the syrup to cool, and then strain it through a muslin cloth. Store in the fridge.

** To preserve rhubarb: place chunks of rhubarb with some home-made vanilla syrup (use the recipe above, but omit the orange and ginger) and a small cooked beetroot (for colour) in an air-tight container. Store the container in the fridge for 24 hours, and then remove the beetroot. Your preserved rhubarb chunks will last for approximately seven days. Visit www.gingarden.com for more detailed instructions.

Serves 1

50ml (2fl oz) **rhubarb vodka**

15ml (½fl oz) **lemon juice**

15ml (½fl oz) home-made **vanilla, ginger and orange syrup***

5 pieces of **preserved rhubarb**** (approximately 1-cm chunks)

5 **rose petals** cut into chiffonade

4 **mint leaves** cut into chiffonade

Sparkling mineral water

1 fresh **rhubarb** strip, to garnish

Rosa damascena aromatic rose water to spritz (optional)

Rheubarbarum Verum

Rhubarb (*Rheum rhaponticum*) from Kircher: *China Monumentis*, 1667.

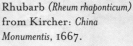

LEVANTINE FIZZ

A toast to the Levantines and the flavours they have collected and dispersed. The scent of spring evenings around the Mediterranean, orange blossom provides a subtle aromatic note. The green cardamon tempers the headiness of the orange blossom and the richness of full-fat yogurt. This luscious combination of aromatic flavours encased in silky bubbles is perfect for a languorous afternoon or evening with friends to share the shaking.

Serves 2

1 **egg white*** (from medium sized egg)

1 shot glass **caster sugar**

1 shot glass **thick plain yogurt**

3 shot glasses **cardamom vodka****

1 shot glass freshly squeezed **lemon juice**

1 tsp **orange blossom water**

5 **ice cubes**

soda water to top up glasses

1. Use a shot glass to measure the quantities. Put the egg white and caster sugar in a Boston cocktail shaker (or you can use a 700-ml/1¼-pint jam jar with a lid) and shake for approximately 1 minute until the mixture has formed a foam.

2. Add in the yogurt, cardamom vodka, lemon juice, orange blossom water and ice cubes, then continuously shake until all the ice has melted, at which point you will no longer hear ice rattling inside the shaker. This takes approximately 2–5 minutes. If you prefer, you can use freshly made cardamom tea instead of the cardamom vodka.

3. Divide the mixture between two tall glasses (about 300ml/10 fl oz), and top them up with soda water. Add straws – if you have shaken the drink hard enough, the straws will stand upright in the foam.

*If you wish to avoid consuming raw egg use an extra half shot of yoghurt and half a shot of water instead, but the mixture will not be as bubbly. Just put all the ingredients in together at once, apart from the soda water. Shake until the ice has melted, then pour into the glass and top up with soda water.

** To make cardamom vodka: lightly crush 50 green cardamom pods and leave to steep in 500ml/18 fl oz of vodka for at least 24 hours. If you prefer, you can use freshly made cardamom tea instead. To make this lightly crush 6 cardamom pods, place them in a mug, top up with boiling water and leave to infuse for at least 20 minutes.

Orange Blossom (*Citrus* x *aurantium*) 'Orange Flowers and Fruits, painted in Teneriffe' (Plate 520) by Marianne North.

The LEVANT is a term used to refer loosely to the eastern Mediterranean region in Asia and the north east of Africa and includes Cyprus, Turkey, Syria, Lebanon, Palestine, Israel, Jordan and Egypt. As a region defined by the sea, and with a culture thriving on the international alliance of France and the Ottoman Empire, the Levant fostered a culinary legacy that grew and travelled, thanks to maritime mobility. Yogurt based drinks such as Arabic *leben* and Turkish *ayran* are found across the Levant. In Turkey, *ayran* can be bought in cartons, made at home or, most spectacularly, enjoyed served up icy cold in a tall glass as a towering cloud of bubbles that rise above the rim of the glass.

THE GREAT BRITISH BAKEWELL

With a bow to the traditional Bakewell tart, this fruity concoction is ideal to serve to guests at a barbecue or as an aperitif before dinner.

Serves 6

60g (2¼oz) **raspberries**
1 **peach**, halved and de-stoned
40ml (1½fl oz) **amaretto**
1 x 750ml (1½pt) bottle of
  dry white wine
crushed ice

1. Put the raspberries in a small bowl with one half of the peach. Add the amaretto and, using a hand blender, process to a smooth purée.
2. Pass the purée through a fine sieve into a bowl. Then pour the purée into a chilled carafe or jug, add the wine and stir well to mix.
3. Place a small handful of crushed ice into each of six wine glasses, and pour over the fruit-flavoured wine.
4. Cut the remaining peach half into six wedges, anchor a piece onto the rim of each glass and serve.

Raspberries (*Rubus idaeus*) from
Müller: *Flora Danica*, 1782.

FENNEL

by Susanne Masters

Spice of angels and seeds of desolation. Fennel has appeared in different guises around the globe from arid central Asian plateaus to tropical Brazil. With a recorded history spanning millennia the best place to start unravelling the journeys of fennel are texts written by the Hittites who dominated Anatolia, now known as the Asian part of Turkey, in 1600 BC.

As the Hittites expanded their empire in the Ancient Middle East, they cursed cities that they had conquered and destroyed. Hittite texts from Anatolia refer to seeds of *'marashanha'* being used in the city-cursing ritual conducted to ensure that the city remained uninhabited. An archaeological, linguistic, botanical and ethnobotanical trail led to identifying mysterious *'marashanha'* as fennel (*Foeniculum vulgare*). *'Marashanha'* is an Anatolian word believed to share its origins with the Greek word for fennel. A fragment of cuneiform text notes that *'marashanha'* was used as a food and medicine as well as the seeds of desolation. Out of the types of plants in the region known as fennel, including different species of *Foeniculum*, *Ferula* and *Ferulago*, *Foeniculum vulgare* is the species that can be used as a food and also has properties that symbolise lifeless places. Indeed, it is poisonous to livestock, and was used as a contraceptive. Additionally, it is a plant that is characteristic of deserted habitation, springing up where ground has been disturbed and depleted. Casting seeds of a plant that haunted abandoned sites and could induce death and barrenness in animals and people was symbolic of the subsequent sterility intended for the sites of conquered cities.

Fennel's medicinal properties were not only known to the Hittites: drinking fennel tea to encourage milk production for breast-feeding is still common among many mothers in Europe. Traditional Chinese medicine makes use of fennel for breast-feeding mothers and for the treatment of bronchitis

Fennel
Foeniculum vulgare

Fennel
Foeniculum vulgare

and intestinal complaints. Fennel is also part of the plant pharmacopoeia in Brazil's cultural melting pot, where it is used as a sedative, laxative and to treat bronchitis.

Fennel is one of the plants used to make absinthe that endows the beverage of Parisian bohemians with a property on the cutting edge of nanotechnology. Trans-anethol is a molecule that dominates the flavour of fennel seed. It is soluble in alcohol but hydrophobic (it repels water). When water is added to absinthe, a cloudy layer is formed where the two clear liquids meet. As more water is added, the mixture becomes opaque – the louche effect. What the eye sees as cloudy is the emulsification of tiny droplets of hydrophobic molecules.

Culinary uses of fennel abound. Perhaps fennel as a food has been mastered best by the Italians who use the swollen stems as a vegetable, seeds as a spice and pollen as a flavour so sublime it is called the spice of angels. Fennel pollen is either an expensive culinary ingredient to buy, or is time consuming for a forager to collect. It works exquisitely as a rich flavour reminiscent of fennel seed but is less 'aniseedy'. The flowers can be shaken laboriously into a container to collect the 'pollen', which consists of both pollen and the tiny petals of fennel flowers. A quicker way to collect fennel pollen is to pick the flower heads and leave them to dry, away from light, on rack over a flat tray. In a warm place within a couple of days the fennel pollen will have dropped off and can easily be poured into a container for storing. Fennel flower flavour is well showcased in fennel flower liqueur; yellow and aromatic, it is a smooth digestive at the end of a meal or, over ice, a refreshing tot for hot afternoons.

Italian immigrants took fennel to the USA, where it thrives to the extent that it is considered a highly invasive and problematic species in some states. Similarly, fennel is also an invasive species in Australia.

Fennel was an ancient introduction to the British flora, brought by the Romans as part of their culinary repertoire. Pollen records show early traces of fennel in Roman ruins. Now, it is widespread on roadsides, seashores and wastelands – open places with disturbed ground and conditions reminiscent of its Anatolian

Fennel (*Foeniculum vulgare*) from Thomé: *Flora von Deutschland Österreich und der Schweiz*, Vol. 3, 1885.

origins. It is a well-travelled plant because it is a useful species that has been deliberately taken by people outside of its natural range. Used on its own or as part of a blend of ingredients in tea, fennel is appreciated for its flavour and therapeutic properties. It is an essential ingredient in countless alcoholic beverages, including spiced liqueurs and gin. Fennel is a visually discrete plant with diminutive flowers and insubstantial, seemingly finely divided leaves. Yet, its humble appearance belies its history as the plant that was once used to curse cities.

Tab. 107

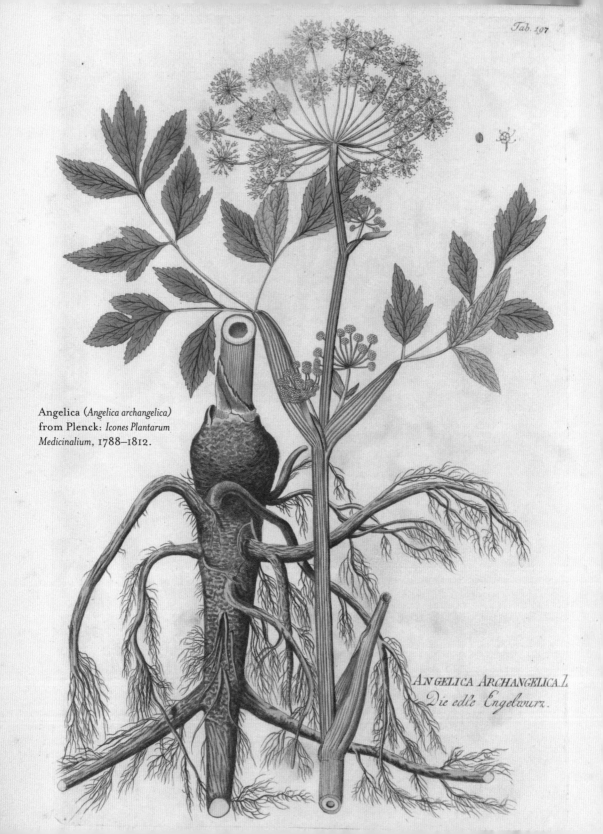

Angelica (*Angelica archangelica*)
from Plenck: *Icones Plantarum
Medicinalium*, 1788–1812.

ANGELICA ARCHANGELICA L.
Die edle Engelwurz.

SHORTS AND TIPPLES

Fig.1. **PRUNUS** spinosa. **PRUNIER** épineux.

Fig.2. **PRUNIER** de Saint - Julien.

Sloes (*Prunus spinosa*) from Duhamel du Monceau: *Traité des arbres et arbustes*, Vol. 5, 1812.

FENNEL FLOWER LIQUEUR

Visit an Italian house and if you are lucky a bottle of homemade liqueur will be pulled out of the freezer. Limoncello is the internationally famous, freezer-dwelling, Italian liqueur, but there are many regional variations and individual creativity produces a myriad of liqueurs in different flavours. While fennel leaves can be picked nearly all year round and fennel seeds retain their flavour while waiting in store cupboards, the flavour of fennel flowers fades relatively quickly. This liqueur captures the essence of summertime in southern Italy.

Makes about 1 litre (1¾pt)

40 **fennel flower heads**, freshly picked

400ml (15fl oz) **95° alcohol**, or 1 litre (1¾pt) **vodka**

600ml (1pt) **water**

300g (10oz) **caster sugar**

To serve:
ice cubes (optional)
soda water (optional)
orange peel (optional)

1. Remove as much of the flower stalks as possible. This is most easily done by holding the flowers of one head together and pulling off the stalks.

2. Put the flower heads and the alcohol (or vodka) in a large jar (a Kilner jar is ideal) just big enough to contain the liquid, and seal it with an airtight lid. Leave the mixture to infuse for 10 days. Give the jar a shake each day if possible.

3. If you have used alcohol, strain the fennel-flower-infused alcohol into a large jug and combine it with the water and sugar. If you have used vodka, strain the infused vodka into a large jug and combine it only with the sugar. Decant the liqueur into bottles with leak-proof caps.

4. The liqueur is best served after it has been chilled in the freezer as an icy shot. For a longer, more contemplative, drink, pour a large shot of the liqueur over a generous handful of ice, or serve with ice, soda water and a twist of orange peel.

Pick fennel flowers on a dry sunny day. There should be plenty of insects hovering about the flowers and feeding on them. If the flowers are not good enough for insects, it is not worth picking them for your kitchen. Individual fennel flowers are so tiny that they would defy picking each one singly. Conveniently for foragers, these flowers are arranged in umbels. In an umbel, the stem of each flower radiates out from the same point on stems of approximately equal length, like the ribs of an umbrella. To pick one head of fennel flowers, simply snap off the stem leading to what looks like an umbrella composed of lots of little umbrellas. Do not wash the fennel flowers — if you do you will be washing the flavour off. Make sure they are clean enough for consumption by picking them away from roadsides and other sources of pollution. In the UK, the best place to find fennel is along seashores.

LOGANBERRY VODKA

Good for sore throats, this luscious winter warmer is a great way to use up surplus soft fruit — and a very nice drink for any occasion. You can use any ripe soft fruit such as loganberries, raspberries or strawberries. The time taken to make the drink makes it an ideal winter drink or to give as a Christmas present, if you can bear to part with it!

1. Place the soft fruit in the bottom of a large glass container, a demijohn is ideal, but a large glass jar will do. Cover the fruit with a decent layer of sugar.
2. Add the vodka at a ratio of approximately 4:1 by volume. For example, if your glass container is 20 per cent full with fruit and sugar, fill the remaining 80 per cent with vodka.
3. Seal the jar, and leave it somewhere that is cool and dark for at least three months. The longer you leave it, the stronger the fruit taste.
4. Shake the container gently every couple of weeks to mix the ingredients well. After three months, strain off the liquid through a layer of muslin or a 'jelly bag'. The liquid can be poured straight into bottles, labelled and stored in a cool, dark place. The vodka will form a layer of sediment in the bottom of the bottle, so decant it before drinking. Although you can drink it after three months, it is best after about six months. You can also use the remaining alcohol-infused fruit on puddings or with ice-cream, but beware it can be very potent!

For quantities, see method

loganberries or other soft fruit, picked over to remove any leaves, bad fruit or other debris

granulated sugar

vodka

Loganberry (*Rubus*) from Hedrick: *The Small Fruits of New York*, 1925.

VIOLET RESTORATIVE

A traditional family tonic in Bob Flowerdew's household, this is apparently a reputed aphrodisiac, as well as being a cure-all. Taken for sore throats, to combat a cold or chill or just as a pick-me-up you can also enjoy the sheer pleasure of the gorgeous aroma.

Makes approximately 450ml (16fl oz)

1,000 **sweet violet petals**
   (yes, it does say 1,000)
150ml (¼pt) **white rum**,
   preferably over-proof
240ml (8fl oz) **water**
150g (5oz) **caster sugar**

1. Pick fresh purple violet petals, and immediately nip off the white base of each, as that part is bitter.
2. Add the purple petals to a large, clean glass jar (such as a Kilner jar) containing the rum. Leave the jar in a cool, dark place for two weeks, but give it a gentle shake daily.
3. Boil the water, add sugar, and stir until dissolved. Then leave to cool (some sugar may crystallise, but that is not a problem). Strain the petals from the rum, then mix the rum and sugar solution and bottle. Keep it in a cool, dark cupboard until it is required. It should be consumed by the teaspoonful, sipped slowly and not swallowed in one gulp.

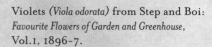

Violets *(Viola odorata)* from Step and Boi: *Favourite Flowers of Garden and Greenhouse*, Vol.1, 1896-7.

Violet
Viola

SLOE GIN

Sloe gin is a classic tipple, and the gathering of the fruit from rural hedgerows in October is a lovely excuse to go for a country walk and make the most of shorter daylight hours as winter approaches. It is traditional, but not necessary, to wait until after the first frost to gather sloes. In September you can also find bullaces, wild damsons or plums. This recipe will work equally well with these fruits.

1. Wash the sloes and throw away any rotten ones. Prick each fruit in several places with a pin. A clever way to do this efficiently is to to make yourself a 'pin-pad', by pushing 6 or more pins through a thin rubber eraser that you can then use to prick a number sloes at one time. Alternatively, you can freeze the sloes thoroughly, then thaw them. This tends to perforate their skins which has the same effect.

2. Place the sloes into the jar, add the sugar and then the gin, up to the rim. Use the full amount of sugar for a sweeter tasting end result, less if you prefer your gin a little dry.

3. Seal the jar and shake to help dissolve the sugar. Shake every day until the sugar has disappeared, then store in a cool dark place.

4. After 3 months open the jar and strain the gin through muslin and into sterilised bottles. Discard the fruit. You can drink the gin at this stage but it improves greatly if kept for 12 months.

Makes about 1 litre (1¾pt)

500g (1lb) **sloes**

100-175g (4-6oz) **sugar**

about 750ml (1¼pt) of medium quality **gin**

1 litre **Kilner jar**, or similar with airtight lid

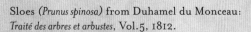

Sloes (*Prunus spinosa*) from Duhamel du Monceau: *Traité des arbres et arbustes*, Vol.5, 1812.

GINGER GIN

Tim Utteridge, who provided this recipe, describes it as a 'very sweet fiery liqueur that is great over ice after dinner', so something to be taken in small quantities and savoured.

Makes approximately 1 bottle

1 x 350g (12oz) jar **stem ginger**
1 x 700ml (1⅛pt) bottle of **gin** or **vodka**

Chop up the stem ginger and place the ginger and the syrup from the jar in a large container that has a top. Add the bottle of gin or vodka. Cover, and leave the mixture to infuse for at least a month.

Ginger (*Zingiber officinale*) from Köhler: *Medizinal Pflanzen*, 1883–1914.

RASPBERRY GIN

Megan Gimber also recommends infusing gin with raspberries. It can be drunk as a liqueur, or used as the basis for a beautiful variation on the traditional gin and tonic combination.

Fill a large jar (one that has an airtight lid, a Kilner jar is ideal) with ripe raspberries, and top up with the gin of your choice. Shake the jar and leave the mixture to infuse for at least a month. Use as desired.

Makes 1 jar
raspberries
gin

Raspberry
Rubus idaeus

HONEY GIN

This is Megan Gimber's tasty infusion recipe that combines honey and gin. If you don't have access to honeycomb, then a few tablespoons of nice honey will do the trick instead.

Makes 1 jar

a 7.5cm (3in) square piece of **honeycomb**, scored
gin

Place the honeycomb in a large jam jar (one that has an airtight lid, a Kilner jar is ideal), and top up with the gin of your choice. Shake the jar and leave the mixture to infuse for at least a month. Serve over ice as an after-dinner liqueur.

Bee balm (*Monarda didyma*) from Miller:
Illustratio systematis sexualis Linnaei, 1804.

NOYAU-BEECH LEAF LIQUEUR

For an unusual and rather different tipple, head outside at the end of April and find a beech tree. Pick the young leaves (they should still be light green, a little downy and not yet waxy).

Makes approximately 1 litre (1¾ pints)

400g (14oz) young fresh
   beech leaves

1 x 700ml (1⅛pt) bottle of **gin**

300g (10oz) **caster sugar**

1. Collect enough beech leaves to fill a 1-litre Kilner jar. Fill the Kilner jar with beech leaves, pressing them down to get as many in as possible. The more you include, the better the end result. Leave a finger's width of space at the top.

2. Fill the jar with gin, making sure that all the leaves are covered by the liquid. This is important because it will ensure that the gin has a nice light green colour. Close the lid on the jar, and leave it in a dark place for two weeks.

3. Pour 200ml (7fl oz) of water into a medium-sized saucepan and add the sugar and heat until the sugar is dissolved.

4. Strain the gin, and wait for the syrup to cool. Once the syrup is cool, mix it with the gin and bottle. Serve over ice for a deliciously herby and nutty after-dinner drink.

Beech
Fagus

VIOLETTE VOULAN'S VIN DE NOIX

This recipe for walnut wine has been passed down a Provençal farming family from one generation to the next. Patience is required, along with freshly picked walnuts, but the result is a silky, delicious *vin de noix*. It's a gorgeous aperitif, fragrant and sweet, that can be enjoyed all year round. The sunrise harvest is probably optional, but Violette would argue that it contributes to the pomp and ceremony of this annual ritual for her and her life companion Maxime Rimbert.

1. At sunrise, on the feast day of St John (24 June), pick 39 walnuts, which should still be in their green outer skin. If they are on the small side, pick an extra five.
2. Without removing the green outer skin, quarter the walnuts using a knife – they are of course still soft at this stage – and drop them into a clean, 10-litre demijohn (or any other large container with a lid).
3. Add the red wine, eau-de-vie, vanilla, orange and cinnamon. Put a stopper on the demijohn (or cover on the container) and leave the mixture to macerate during the summer.
4. In September, add the sugar and roll or shake the demijohn to ensure that the sugar dissolves. Then strain the wine immediately into bottles. The bottles should be left as long as possible for the wine to mature, but there is no harm in opening one at Christmas. Serve in small glasses as an aperitif.

Makes approximately 7 x 750ml bottles

39 **walnuts** in their green outer skin

5 litres (8¾ pints) approximately 7 x 750 ml bottles good quality **red wine**, such as Côtes du Ventoux

1 litre (1¾ pt) **eau-de-vie**, 50% proof

1 **vanilla pod**

Peel of 1 small **orange**, preferably dried

1–2 small pieces **cinnamon bark**

1kg (2lb) **white refined sugar**

A 10 litre **demijohn** (or other large container with a lid)

Walnut (*Juglans regia*) from Duhamel du Monceau: *Traité des arbres et arbustes*, 1755.

RATAFIA OF BLACKCURRANTS

A ratafia is a sweet, fortified wine that was popular in the 19th century in Mediterranean countries such as Spain and Italy, as well as parts of France. This recipe comes from Peter Jonas's 1818 book, *The Distiller's Guide*. The quantities are the original ones, but you may prefer to reduce them as you wish, unless you are making bottles to give away as presents.

**Makes approximately
5.5 litres (10 pints)**

2kg (4lb) **blackcurrants**

1kg (2lb) **morello cherries**

500g (1lb) **blackcurrant
    leaves**

1 tsp **cloves**

5.5 litres (10 pt) **brandy**

4.5kg (10lb) **caster sugar**

1. Crush the fruit and strain it through a sieve.
2. Put the fruit, leaves, cloves, brandy and sugar in a demijohn or large jar (alternatively, divide the quantities equally between several large jars) with an airtight lid, and leave to infuse for one month.
3. After a month, filter the ratafia and pour into bottles and keep. You can drink it straightaway, or store it in a cool, dark place.

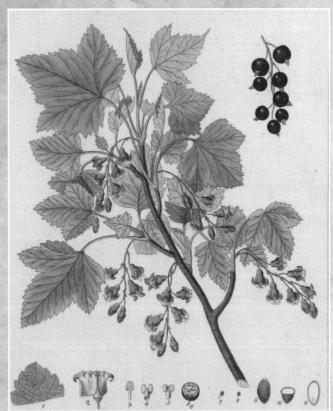

Blackcurrent (*Ribes nigrum*) from Hayne: *Getreue darstellung und beschreibung der in der arzneykunde gebräuchlichen gewächse*, 1805-9.

MRS BEETON'S CHERRY BRANDY

Making preserves and pickling vegetables was an important task in Victorian households. Cooks were adept at conjuring up recipes to cope with a glut of one foodstuff or another. This recipe for cherry brandy is ideal for making something a little special if you have cherries to spare.

1. You will need one or two (possibly more, depending on their capacity) clean, large-necked bottles or jars that are perfectly dry with either cork stoppers or airtight lids. Check the cherries to make sure that they are fresh and not too ripe. Cut off about half the stalks of each.

2. Layer the cherries and the sugar in each bottle or jar until the bottle is almost full. (Don't use too much sugar as it can make the cherries go too hard.) If using, add the apricot kernels or almonds (Mrs Beeton advises that they will 'add much to their flavour'. Then top up with the brandy, leaving a slight gap beneath the bottom of the cork stopper (if using) or the airtight lid.

3. Cork the bottles firmly or put the airtight lid on firmly. If using cork stoppers, Mrs Beeton advised that they should be covered with a 'piece of bladder' which should be tied round the neck of the bottle. Store in a dry place for 2–3 months before using.

Makes approximately
1.1 litres (2pt)

500g (1lb) **cherries**

75g (3oz) **caster sugar**

2 **apricot kernels**, or a handful of **bitter almonds**, blanched (optional)

150ml (5fl oz) **brandy**

Cherry (*Prunus*) from Poiteau:
Pomologie Française, 1846.

FURTHER READING

The Art of Cookery, Made Plain and Easy, By a Lady (Hannah Glasse), 7th edition, A. Millar (1760)
Mrs Beeton's Every Day Cookery and Housekeeping Book, Ward, Lock & Co (1884 Edition)
Kew's Global Kitchen Cookbook, Kew Publishing (2013)
Hugh Johnson and Jancis Robinson, *The World Atlas of Wine*, 7th Edition, Mitchell Beazley (2013)
Peter Jonas, *The Distiller's Guide*, Sherwood, Neely, and Jones, and Dring and Fage (1816)
Lynn Parker and Kiri Ross-Jones, *The Story of Kew Gardens in Photographs*, Arcturus Publishing (2013)
Jean Pettigrew, *A Social History of Tea*, National Trust (2001)
Jerry Thomas, *The Bar-tenders Guide, or How to Mix all Kinds of Fancy Drinks*, Dick & Gerald (1876)

Publisher's note about plant names
The classification of plants is constantly being amended with the advancement of scientific research. We have used current scientific names in picture captions in the book, hence is the reason why some names differ from those on the actual illustration.

CREDITS

p37 Queen's Garden, Kew by Rachel Warne
p61 Zoffany, Royal Collection Trust
p73 Hunte's Gardens, Barbados by Mike Beament

Woodcuts are taken from:
Gerard: *The Herball or Generall Historie of Plantes*, 1597.
Culpeper: *The Complete Herbal*, 1653.
Mattioli: *Commentaries in six volumes on De Materia Medica of the Physician Dioscorides of Anazarba*, 1559-1660.

The Publisher would like to thank the following for their help with the editorial development of this project:, Sophie Burgham, Dominica Costello, Jemma Magrath, Daphne Maryanka, Taffy Schneider, Lorna Terry, Lydia White, and the staff of Kew's Library, Art and Archives, especially Fiona Ainsworth, Julia Buckley and Lynn Parker.

ACKNOWLEDGMENTS

Essay Contributors

Caroline Craig is the co-author of *The Little Book of Lunch* and *The Cornershop Cookbook*, published by Square Peg, Random House. She lives in London.

Hattie Ellis is a food writer, author and contributor to Kew magazine, whose books include two on bees and honey. www.hattieellis.com

Bob Flowerdew has written over two dozen gardening books, been presenter for BBC *Gardeners' World* and twenty-two years on BBC Radio 4s *Gardeners' Question Time*.

Gina Fullerlove is Head of Publishing at the Royal Botanic Gardens, Kew.

Susanne Groom is a writer and consultant curator for Historic Royal Palaces.

Sarah Heaton is a city gardener, garden designer and garden writer based in Shepherds Bush, London. http://sarahheatongardens.com

Jason Irving works at Kew on the Medicinal Plant Names Services (MPNS) project, he is also studying for a degree in herbal medicine and leads regular foraging courses in London. www.foragewildfood.com

Sheila Keating is the former food writer of *The Times Magazine* who now concentrates on books, particularly collaborations with leading chefs.

Susanne Masters is a plant scientist who consults on botanical ingredients, travels for orchids, wild swimming and edible adventures. @Ethnobotanica

Sophie Missing is a journalist, editor and author who lives in London. She is the co-author, with Caroline Craig, of *The Little Book of Lunch* and *The Cornershop Cookbook*.

Recipe Contributors

The Royal Botanic Gardens, Kew would like to thank the following for donating their favourite drinks recipes:
Ampersand Caterers: *20 Below, The Walled Garden, Golden Meadows*; Bompas and Parr LLP: *World's Hottest Bloody Maria, Opium Poppy Old Fashioned*; Jared Brown, Master Distiller and the Sipsmith Distillery: *London Punch, Traditional Spice Punch, Spiced Tonic*; Jeremy Cherfas: *Triple C, Warm Mocha Punch*; Max Clark, Leiths School of Food and Wine: *Angel's Breath, Bee Balm Brew, Limoncello Fizz, Marmalade-ade, Masala Chai, Midsummer's Night Tisane, Red Cherry Carnival, Sanguinella Sour, Strawberry Basil and St Germain Crush, The Great British Bakewell, Zesty Pink Grapefruit and Pansy Tea*; Caroline Craig: *Vanilla Chai, Vin de Noix*; Hattie Ellis: *Spiced Fizzy Iced Tea*; Bob Flowerdew: *Eggnog, Violet Restorative, Pear Syrup, Raspberry Syrup*; The Gin Garden: *Paradise Martini, Three Fruit Mary, Rhubarb Rose*; Susanne Groom: *Nettle beer, Caudle, Eighteenth-Century-Style Chocolate, Lemon Barley Water, Whey*; Sarah Heaton: *Basic Fruit Smoothie, Smoothie variations: Banana and Pear, Courgette and Cucumber, Apricot and Almond, Peaches and Cream, Avocado*; Sheila Keating: *Chilli hot chocolate, Coupette No.3, Chilli Martini*; Susanne Masters: *Ottoman Rose Sherbet, Levantine Fizz, Fennel Flower Liqueur*; Sophie Missing: *Winter Spiced Negroni*; Peyton & Byrne: *Berry Spice*; Sarah Raven: *Rhubarb Cordial*; Taylors of Harrogate: *Peppermint Mojito Spritzer, Spiced Apple Spritzer, Sweet Rhubarb Cocktail*.

The Kew Publishing team would like to thank the following staff and volunteers for their recipes:
Mike Beament, (Volunteer, Kew Arboretum): *Hunte's Ginger Lemonade*; Antony Berry (Major Giving Manager): *Peanut Butter and Banana Smoothie, Blueberry Vitality Smoothie;* Lee Davies (Fungarium Collections Assistant): *Elder rob*; Sarah Fardipour (Business Systems Support Officer): *Persian Sweet and Sour Mint and Cucumber Drink*; Jonathon Farley (Senior Conservator): *Norman Court Grog*; Gina Fullerlove (Head of Publishing): *Rum Butter Punch for Twelfth Night, Oma's Whittenham cider, Mulled Wine*; Megan Gimber (former QA officer Digital Collections Unit): *Rhubarb and Elderflower Champagne, Meader, Honey Gin, Raspberry Gin*; Jonathon Kendon (Lab Technician, in vitro biology): *Granny's lemonade*; Katherine O'Donnell (former QA Officer Digital Collections Unit): *Noyau-Beech Leaf Liquor*; Huma Qureshi (Finance Assistant): *Persian Rose Petal Syrup*; Diana Rawlinson (Support team Millennium Seed Bank): *Elderflower Cordial*; Janet Terry (Seed Collections Manager): *Loganberry Vodka*; Tim Utteridge (Assistant Head of Science, Identification & Naming): *Jus Alpokat, Ginger Gin*.

INDEX

CONVERSIONS AND ABBREVIATIONS FOR COMMON MEASURES

Never mix types of measures – always stick to one or another.

Abbreviations used in this book

g	gram
kg	kilogram
ml	millilitre
l	litre
mm	millimetre
cm	centimetre
oz	ounce
lb	pound
fl oz	fluid ounce
pt	pint
tsp	teaspoon
tbsp	tablespoon
mins	minutes
in	inch

Weights

5g	¼ oz
15g	½ oz
20g	¾ oz
25g	1 oz
50g	2 oz
75g	3 oz
100g	4 oz
150g	5 oz
175g	6 oz
200g	7 oz
250g	8 oz
275g	9 oz
300g	10 oz
325g	11 oz
350g	12 oz
375g	13 oz
400g	14 oz
500g	1 lb
1kg	2 lb

US weight equivalents

25g (1oz)	cup
50g (2oz)	¼ cup
100g (4oz)	½ cup
175g (6oz)	¾ cup
250g (8oz)	1 cup
500g (1lb)	2 cups

Measurements

5mm	¼ inch
1cm	½ inch
1.5cm	¾ inch
2.5cm	1 inch
5cm	2 inches
10cm	4 inches
15cm	6 inches
20cm	8 inches
25cm	10 inches
30cm	12 inches

Liquids / volumes

5 ml	¼ fl oz*
15 ml	½ fl oz
25 ml	1 fl oz
45 ml	1½ fl oz
50 ml	2 fl oz
75 ml	3 fl oz
100ml	3½ fl oz
125ml	4 fl oz
150ml	¼ pt
175ml	6 fl oz
200ml	7 fl oz
250ml	8 fl oz
275ml	9 fl oz
300ml	½ pt
350ml	12 fl oz
375ml	13 fl oz
400ml	14 fl oz
450ml	¾ pt
500ml	17 fl oz
600ml	1 pt
750ml	1¼ pt
900ml	1½ pt
1 litre	1¾ pt

*1 teaspoon

Citron (*Citrus medica*) from collection of paintings by Chinese artists, probably early 19th century.